T0367582

ORPHANS OF THE STORM

MARIA DOWNEY

ARCHWAY
PUBLISHING

Archway Publishing books may be ordered through booksellers or by contacting:

Archway Publishing
1663 Liberty Drive
Bloomington, IN 47403
www.archwaypublishing.com
1 (888) 242-5904

ISBN: 978-1-4808-8811-1 (sc)
ISBN: 978-1-4808-8933-0 (hc)
ISBN: 978-1-4808-8812-8 (e)

Library of Congress Control Number: 2020902254

Print information available on the last page.

Archway Publishing rev. date: 3/05/2020

For my Father Al

INTRODUCTION

S outh of the city of Berlin is a newly constructed concentration camp. It houses all the homosexuals exiled to it by the Third Reich. Their goal: to eliminate sodomy by gassing the inhabitants. The German government declares them all degenerate in speeches to the German people, heard on the radio. Germany annihilates two million people immediately.

These German homosexuals are killed within one year's time. This is well before Adolf Hitler has come to power. He is at the time, all of fifteen years, living in a small village.

Later, after Hitler's assassinates the President of Austria on his eighteenth birthday; he and his men take over the Austrian government in a coup d'état. Hitler shoots the

President of Austria, Dollfuss in the head point blank, execution style.

Austria was completely opposed to the Third Reich's incursion into their nation of Austria, by Brown shirts.

The new, self-declared, Chancellor of Germany crowns his own head with a laurel wreath in public view. Stomping his foot in public spectacle; he declares reassuringly to Germans, that he is eliminating degeneracy from his society. Thousands waste away. The arts and culture of Germany are censored continually, by appointed Minister of Propaganda, Josef Goebbels.

Similarly, the contemporary Russian President, Vladimir Putin, has also declared war on homosexuals in Russian held territory.

This now current President, while a former Premier leader of Russia, has deliberately sent firing squads into innumerable nightclubs to murder all homosexuals on sight. It was broadcast by the International Press through Reuters, during the month of August 2013. His hatred of all things homosexual is so notorious in this leader, that he has ordered firing squads to roam the streets near the Black Sea. It was the Winter Olympics 2014, televised internationally on prime time, on International Television stations.

These reports we're televised to the American people, continually, on all networks covering the Winter Olympics. There is no protest from the Russian people. This indicates a willingness, and complicity to purge undesirables, that is startling. There was also a marked lack of cogent response from world leaders which is very telling. A public outcry is necessary to ensure that the concentration camp philosophy, as a way of dealing with undesirables, does not become prevalent once again, under Putin's regime as it was in the 1970's-1980's. That purge cost eight million lives in the Southern provinces.

The commonly used expression "work camps", is an old expression, utilized by the Reich, under Adolf Hitler, to disguise the true intent of these camps to sequester, maim and starve to death by the millions, anyone perceived as different.

In the general scheme of things, silence denotes complicity. How soon we have forgotten the lessons of outright Fascism learned during WWII.

President Vladimir Putin's fear of contracting AIDS is legendary. He takes four to five baths daily in antiseptic wash to ensure long life. His emphasis on health is always picked up by press photographers to depict this leader as physically strong and enduring. He probably thinks it reassures the Russian people. But hysteria over AIDS is a dangerous and potent weapon in the wrong hands. It fuels the fires of suspicion and paranoia among the ignorant. People who reside in small towns, far away from real contemporary health education believe old wives tales, myths which encourage a historical approach to AIDS sufferers. Without proper education by physicians and health professionals, with current updated knowledge on AIDS, the Russians people are susceptible to lies and ridiculous hate mongering in reference to their treatment of AIDs patients. This had created an atmosphere of violence in Russia not seen since 1932.

Why elect a leader, who not only permits hate mongering, suspicion and ignorance of this issue but allows these death camps to flourish unabated in his country? Wiser heads can see that it is devastating to the welfare of Russia in general. These parallels in time are so foreboding.

It is so like Hitler, that essentially President Vladimir Putin is accomplishing the same purge as Adolf Hitler. What is the difference when millions are either shot or starved to death in camps near Saint Petersburg? Young people in Russian and the old satellite countries are raising red flags, questioning this rhetoric of hatred. The camps called strangely, "work camps" we're also present in Russian and Germany during WWII. They were poor excuses for isolating, and sequestering all things homosexual or 'deviant' from the macho Russian society. Joseph Stalin notwithstanding, who purged eight million deviants Russians. They are defined by Lenin as people "Who will not cow tow to the party line such as Jews and Catholics. The fear of AIDS in Russian is so overwhelming that fear has led to complete and total annihilation in Russia, of any and all homosexuals under Putin's Regime re being machine gunned in nightclubs. This was shown on American TV, at the Winter Olympics, on all networks particularly KABC. Nightclubs were labeled by President Putin as decadent filthy places to annihilate. Thousands of young people were gunned down with machine guns sent there in squad cars by President Putin, in full view of the visiting, International Press, stationed near the Black Sea region. Some of this was exposed on Reuters News services. Video was exhibited on American Television. Ignorance of AIDS/SIDAS there is staggering!

Since education is not mandatory in rural area of Russian peasants do not have the latest scientific discoveries about AIDS/SIDAS. This political red herring is being used as an excuse by politicos there, to purge and annihilate all homosexuals in Russian held territories. The situation in Bulgaria and Estonia is so bad, that thousands have been tortured and killed under Putin's orders.

Annihilation of anything different or nonconformist in the Russian viewpoint (for all the world to see), has become commonplace. It is easily forgotten in time by the world's peoples. Why are Americans so sheltered from these harsh realities? Now we have a Dictator named Mr. Vladimir Putin, in Russia, basically participating in the same carnage, the same outrages as before in the 1930's. How can we close our eyes and ears to it? Over seven million persons, at last count, have been thrown into open pits in conquered, Russian territories. It is a purge on a global scale. Why do we ignore these purges? When we turn on out television; we get a thirty second sound blip of international news. We are blinded by our own political censorship of news. It is vital to our decision making powers as a free Republic. We are an educated people. This nation has a higher education standard than any other nation, yet we are being treated like children by the media. Why are we being fed Pablum instead of informative truths in the media? Who decides what we can or cannot view on television? Why do these executives decide that Americans cannot sustain news of tragedies/wars when we offer our own sons, to these wars, to fight on our behalf.

All these things affect our economy and life standards. The government needs to shed light on these wars abroad, so we can grapple with answers to these questions especially now, prior to election time. In Europe the news is open, revealing, and vital to adult viewers after ten o'clock. Why are we being slighted the reality of these incursions, and purges? Americans are hungry for in depth reporting yet we have sound blips of little consequence. When we turn on our television, everything has been dumbed down to the intellectual level of a ten year old! It is an insult to our collective intelligence and consciousness.

My greatest fear is that we are sleeping through an international war of major consequences. There is no moral excuse for our lack of knowledge and silence. This silence is deafening! The blind are leading the blind.

Putin has made no bones about this to the International press

Association. There is no excuse for ignorance about Putin's agenda. It was clearly and bravely covered by the press during the Winter Olympics by the International Press Association. Some journalists have even lost their lives to cover this atrocity.

In Nazi Germany, circa 1932, gays were the first group to be destroyed, gassed in toto by the Third Reichdom. Hitler trained his men to torture and disrespect anyone who did not meet his stringent criteria for the 'perfection" of the German race.

They were so desperate for jobs after the Great Depression, the German people were consumed with wild dreams of wealth. Some stole for a living, while mobsters raided bars, and stole booze. Slowly the German people sought relief from poverty, seeking it in charismatic leaders, who promised them everything, but only gave them only a cheap perfume to gloss over their real problems.

by Maria Therese Downey in the year of our Lord 2016

CONTENTS

Acknowledgments xv

Chapter 1   Cold Cuts 1
Chapter 2   Trout Season 7
Chapter 3   The Hague 13
Chapter 4   Attache 19
Chapter 5   "The Eliminator" 23
Chapter 6   Western Union 31
Chapter 7   Tow Headed Girl 35
Chapter 8   Chow Down 37
Chapter 9   Reconnassaisance 43
Chapter 10 Siena 47
Chapter 11 Tail-Spin 49
Chapter 12 Whitewashed 53
Chapter 13 Alsace Lorraine 59
Chapter 14 Tri-Cornered Hat 63
Chapter 15 Evelyn 65
Chapter 16 Rivers of Fire 75
Chapter 17 Blood Oath 77
Chapter 18 "The "Flying Wallendas." 85
Chapter 19 Blue Chippy 91
Chapter 20 "Nemesis" 97
Chapter 21 Berry-Au-Bac 103

Chapter 22 Lausanne 111
Chapter 23 Kindercamp.. 123

Bibliography.. 125
Personal Statement 127

ACKNOWLEDGMENTS

The impetus of this novel embraces memories told to me by a decorated WWI Corporal. Most of these stories were slowly revealed to me during several lengthy interviews, at the Veterans Memorial Hospital in the Rehabilitation Ward, for wounded Veterans of WWII. This Veteran learned to walk again in physical therapy sessions and Jacuzzi's after substantial injuries to his lower spine.

One of his idols was famous actress Patricia Neal, seen in the film, "Hud," who had to learn to speak again after a traumatic incident. He corresponded with her for years.

This work was compiled over three-year's time, combined with detailed research of the War itself. Other war veterans from France and Germany were also interviewed at length. One focus in these novels are on the Schmidt Clan from Minnesota. They are a group of loyal émigrés, who escaped the genocide due to their Catholicism. They, therefore completely rejected the Reich's ethos under self-proclaimed Chancellor Hitler. This is one reason that the wise, General Eisenhower, sent in Catholic troops first to squelch Hitler's army. French, Italian and German-American soldiers were on the front lines, the bravest of the lot. Their faith was so strong that it made them all the more determined to eliminate the genocide.

My father always said that "It is amazing how quickly soldiers who are Atheists find God, when faced down with a bomb or a machine gun."

This story focuses on the many battles which General's; Patton Eisenhower and Montgomery planned. This Corporal participated in them, under the leadership of General Patton, in North Africa for seventeen years. Patton lead the invasion of Berlin in 1936.

The style of this piece is stream of consciousness, a more Surrealistic style of writing. It includes many vignettes concerning particular individuals involved in WWII. It has a quality of the films made by the inspiring Director, Robert Altman whose unusual technique of subconcial vignettes has influenced filmmakers in the 1970's.

The memoirs of a soldier are reflected here, as a tribute to the hardships which won a victory for the Allies. It is during the "War to end all wars," as Churchill believed. As a decorated WWII Veteran, the Protagonist, Corporal Al Downey, worked for seventeen years closely with General George C. Patton in North Africa near the Sudan. It was during the glory days of the Fighting Third and Fourth Regiments, that he served for the battalion. Patton later swept through Berlin, as this General marched his troops boldly into the center of the melee.

They were stationed in the Sudan for over fifteen years, then finally at General Eisenhower's order they stormed Berlin. Eisenhower said that he would "Send the biggest SOB in Berlin to squelch the Nazi's at the "Reichtung." It drew the war to a close in Western Europe, overturning the AXIS Powers, liberating Dachau and Auschwitz Concentration camps. The horrors of those camps remained with my father the rest of his life. His traumas were often spoken of but never written down. Like most Vets, he could not verbalize the horrors. He himself was captured during an operation to airlift orphans from Rome during the "Seven Percent Solution." He was imprisoned near the French Border in Germany for six months; tortured in an Officer's Prison Camp; then liberated by the French troops. Near the end of the war much to his chagrin, he decided to rejoin General Patton to invade Berlin. It had become crucial to him, as well as his view of himself as an Irish-American soldier. Marching through the Arc D'Triomphe on "D" Day was finally liberating for him.

"Man's inhumanity to man," was something which haunted him until he died, a famous quote by Thomas Mann. When he passed away in 1989; he had written several speeches as a ghost writer for; President

Lyndon Baines Johnson and President John Fitzgerald Kennedy, affectionately called "The Fitz", as well as Dr. Martin Luther King Jr. He also was responsible for the writing of the screenplay for Warner Brothers. "Patton" starring George C. Scott, playing the effusive General, which packed a wallop.

The opening speech was his 'pride and joy". Some of these memories are harsh, and to the modern eye, seem almost impossible to trust. However, they are true accounts of the times from 1932-1942. He also wrote "April in Paris" about "The Lost Generation," of Americans, who swarmed to Paris, disillusioned and broken, after the battles were done.

Thankfully my father, did manage to return home safely, albeit in a wheelchair for four years. His rehabilitation in the Veteran's Hospital taught him how to walk all over again. When he finally got off his crutches, all he wanted to do was dance with my mother Katherine. They were married for forty-nine years. So here's a toast to you guys! Slainshe!

COLD CUTS

South Gate is the old gate to the Orange Grove, owned by the Medusa Family of Spain. It is now bordered by the Santa Fe Railroad. In the 1800's, the train cars hauled orange crates teeming with produce, through the midlands to the San Francisco Bay region.

On the corner of Firestone lies a stately, yellow house. Behind the Medieval looking brick fence of twelve feet high, with built in fireplace, lies a tennis, court surrounded by bougainvillea's, morning glories and snapdragons.

This is a place of refuge for a Post War family. It is owned proudly by a Veteran, seeking solace. He left the battlefields of this world which were painted with blood. Thousands of American men were sent home, psychologically deranged and physically handicapped. He refers to himself the rest of his life as, "The Prodigal Son," returning home. The war has left dad frustrated, delusioned and bewildered. He says he only wanted to come home every day to see his children. That's what it is all about for him.

This tennis court was his pride and joy. It reminds him so much of the Kennedy's estates. It represents something that he wanted to aspire to. He admired these men so much. It is fronted by a huge, oak tree with a small treehouse resting in the nook of the branches.

There inside a whitewashed porch on a veranda, sit two old buddies, Al and Pete. Pete smokes a hand rolled Havana, blowing smoke rings in the air with purpose. They plan a fishing trip up to San Bernardino Mountains that weekend. They have not told the girls yet. As they plan the supplies, ammunition, rifles etc. to load up in the old Chevy,

Katy offers them a tray of lemonade. "Thanks sweetheart," as Al downs his glass in two gulps. The air is thick with humidity. Katy wipes her hands on her apron, closing the screen door on the porch." I'll just leave you two alone to catch up." She retreats to the back kitchen to prepare cold cuts. The dinner bell is always rung precisely at 1500 on weekends. Orderves are sorely missed unless served first in the living room. Plates of crudité, with fresh salads are served on a Lazy Susan. A lively discussion takes place before dinner. Conversation, usually politically inclined, permeates this home. Al has even run for Mayor of Los Angeles pitting himself against Sam Yorty, the perennial incumbent. Yorty is controlled by so many gangsters it's pathetic. Al Downey garners 20% of the vote, Downtown Los Angeles. This gives him a political power base in the Senate in Sacramento, to negotiate bills. Later he moves up to the Congress to replace an absentee Congressman due to a stroke he suffers. This is for the twenty-fifth Congressional District in Mississippi. He serves the remainder of his term in Washington D.C. by taking the place of an absentee Congressman. For two years, as a Proxy, Al works many long hours in Congress, on the explicit advice of Sargent Shriver who is intermittently in Washington D.C. Shriver fronts the Headstart Program in Mississippi to feed children, down South, healthy breakfasts. He works closely with Stokely Carmichael and Huey Newton in Alabama, Mississippi and parts of Louisiana. Many of these children would have no food at all in the rural, Southern Cross all day long, as sharecropper's children.

Sargent Shriver was the long-term amour of Al's sister, Esther Downey for eight years. They married in Nantucket Bay at Saint Augustine Church. It was annulled by Pope John XXIII in three years, due to the fact that she was barren and incapable of giving birth. Shriver traveled to Rome insisting on the annulment. It broke Esther's heart. She changed her name to Esther Blodgett dropping out of sight. Then she took the veil as Sister Mary Agnes in Fargo, North Dakota. She remained cloistered the rest of her life.

Katy, Al's wife, was shocked at their annulment. She loved Shriver so much, she argued with him to distraction. My Great Uncle was released from responsibilities in 1964, from Al's only sister. In only one year he was engaged to JFK's Aunt Eunice Shriver. They adopted children due to her severe mental retardation. Shriver wanted a house full of children. He continued to visit us. Frequently he gave Al political advice. They enjoyed many conversations, both in Los Angeles and at the White House in Washington D.C., where Al served as Security Advisor to President Lyndon Baines Johnson. Al frequently visited the White House during the Kennedy Administration working with both JFK and Bobby.

Al is listed five times in the Congressional Record for his work in Congress. Al uses this power base to push Civil Rights Bills through the Senate from 1962-1968.

Al has two lively children; David his only son and Maria his only, adopted daughter. He worked with her mother Therese whom he causally called his" sis", an Irish expression which is not familial, at MGM studios. She acted as a "B" movie actress under many pseudonyms from age eight. However, she met a handsome British Officer in New Orleans daring the filming of an MGM picture there. Nine months later giving birth to Maria at age sixteen. Although working, she had to be convinced, by Al in Louisiana, during the filming of "High Society "to give her daughter to his family. His wife was reluctant to take on another child. Sweet Lorraine has a bit part in this film starring; Bing Crosby, Grace Kelly and Satchmo. A private discreet adoption took place when Maria was nearly four years of age. Her birthdate was changed in order to make her the 'kid' sister.

Dave keeps throwing a baseball at the concrete wall out back, bouncing it into his catcher's mitt. He keeps this going for hours. His plans to be a professional ball player are deeply instilled in him, thanks to Coach Wilkerson, who has pushed Dave in Little League towards that goal. All Dave thinks about are his trophies in the glass cabinet, near the bay window. Al and Pete decide to break the news about their fishing, taking off for three days. Katy is so relieved to have the house to herself it's humorous. So the old blue and white Chevy sputters to takeoff.

While they are gone, Dave decides it's the opportune time to run off. He's so feed up with dad's temper, he dons his blue windbreaker heading out to the great unknown. At age eleven, he plans to conquer the world. He gets as far, as the local liquor store. He puts on his navy, windbreaker tearing out of there.

Over the backyard fence is heard 'Come home, I still love you," Katy 'Oh heck, he didn't hear me," she wipes her hands on her apron frustrated. She shouts out at the back fence. "Don't forget dinnertime." He jumps the back brick gate with athletic skill. The girls in the back of the house don't notice anything for hours on end. As darkness falls, there is no Dave around. Maria gets concerned about her brother. She puts on her red, plaid, woolen coat knocking on every door of every friendly person in the neighborhood asking about Dave. She ends up in Mrs. Kolars' house, a Hungarian war refugee, eating freshly baked chocolate chip cookies with cold milk.

This is a clever lady, worried; she senses danger. Maria continues knocking on doors until sundown. Katy has a metal triangle out back which she rings to get her kids back home.

After a restless dinner in the kitchen, Maria insists on running down the street, but is halted by Katy for the night. "Leave him alone and he will come home, wagging his tail behind him,' Katy insists. Three days pass by slowly.

Again Maria insists on finding him. She runs all the way down to the liquor store on the corner. She sees twelve neighbor boys, older teens, clumping together. They disperse as they see her running up, "It's Alma. Scram!' one shouts at them all. This clump of thugs disperses in ten seconds. She thinks it funny that all these big guys, smoking on the corner, run off as she approaches him. She didn't realize that she is his only witness.

Just a little girl in a pink t-shirt with blue-jean overalls runs to the curb to claim her big brother. Dave is crouched over at the waist, seated at the edge of the pavement. Blood is running down his windbreaker. He clutches at his stomach in obvious pain. They had all jumped him. He was the Catholic kid in their hood.

This Protestant gang has a good time shit kicking Dave in the stomach after punching him out. They shit kicked him endlessly until he curled up. "Get out of our hood, you mutherfucker. Don't come back or you get this." One of them put his hand in his coat pocket to indicate a gun. Dave had left an abusive dad to be beaten to a pulp around the corner.'

Maria sits next to him, on the ground, handing him a white hand-kerchief to sop up the blood on his face. "Can you stand up at all? Maria glares at his windbreaker. "Mom will kill you when she sees all this blood on your clothes. What happened Dave? She tries to get him to stand, but he can barely lift himself.

"You're so heavy Dave. Here put your arm on my shoulder." She tries to get him away from this gang as soon as possible. It seems like an endless walk back to the house, down an endless row of tree lined streets. A few neighbors glance out their windows as these two children struggle to get home. They stop repeatedly. He heaves a deep sigh. Dave is so embarrassed that the neighbors will glare at him in defeat. Afraid of his father's wrath he hesitates to go home. He keeps saying, "Why go home when all he'll do is yell at me Ria? "Don't be ridiculous. You can't survive on the street. You're just a kid. What would you do for a living at age twelve? Anyway, where would I be without my big brother?" Maria is so worried he'll run again. Limping along, these two damaged children eventually make it back to the huge, yellow house on the corner. They collapse on the front lawn glaring at the neighborhood. It is stone, cold silent.

TROUT SEASON

Pete and Al arrive around three p.m. in a blue Ford, smelling for all the world of fish. When they exit the vehicle. They drag about seven, enormous trout onto the front lawn to display them. These fish weigh about twenty kilos each. As they lay them on an emerald, green lawn, the neighbor boys begin to circle around Southern Avenue spying the catch, with their bicycles. "Go ask your mother's if they want some trout!" Al shouts happily. Some of them race home. Maria and Dave run out. Maria is still in her overalls as usual. Dave changed into a Hawaiian shirt, his other was so bloody. Katy told him they could not save the windbreaker.

Dave is curious as Pete takes out a buoy knife to cut open the fish." I can teach you how to clean this fish kids," he smiles making a deep incision in the belly of the trout. Dave digs his scout knife into the trout's eye holding it up grimacing. "Have some trout sis", chiding her.

"Now cut that out Dave, or she'll never eat a bite,' Pete glares at him. "No thanks", says Maria as she scrambles off to climb the Cypress tree. "Chicken!" yells Dave. "Who wants to cut an ole fish?" says she.

"Any of you boys want a trout dinner?" Al questions the gathering passel of lads. One boy, Robert Burns, dismounts his bicycle, 'I'll take some Mr. Downey. My dad just lost his job. We sure could use some. We can't afford meat for dinner anymore. Robert Burns was about ten years old. He runs over to Al.

Al and Pete select the best frying fish, wrapping it up in tin foil. Robert Burns is so overjoyed; he runs the fish fry back home. He even leaves his bike on our lawn for awhile.

Pete was dad's oldest friend. He had been with him in Europe in the fighting Third regiment. Pete was a wise, Cherokee Indian from the Lake Huron area. For Al it was a place of peace among the deluge. The war had made Katy's sister a widow. She lost the only man that she would truly love in England. He was a fighter ACE. He went down trapped, inside his MIG, crashing into the sea. It exploding into a ring of fire; the metal pieces flying outward.

England is filled with orphans and widows from the "Blitz". At one point in Rome they were heavily embattled. Running close behind each other, Corp.Al had tripped on a land mine, exploding under the sand. The shrapnel flew up his back. The metal pieces burroughing into his lower spine. He has incapacitated for weeks. Pete got him out of there before all hell broke loose. It opened up a way to go home. However, he landed in Paris instead for five years' time, at the Hospital American, then working with the French Underground.

Kathryn 's family had fled in 1921 from Alsace Lorraine, with a full complement of brothers and sisters, as many as they could round up before the war broke out. Her father Harry Schmidt, was one of thirteen children. They all got out prior to the "New Republic" under Hitler. Later five of them went back at the height of this war, to give Hitler back some hell!

Their family had fled Alsace at the base of the mountains, the border between Switzerland, Spain and German territories. Due to severe, virulent prejudice against their Catholic clan of twenty-three individuals, who opposed the Weimar Republic; they fled with the shirts on their backs. It was through the mountains of the Alsacean region through Spain and then France, making their way to England by ferry boat. After their departure they went through immigration on New York's, Ellis Island.

There had been stirrings of Fascism in the 1930's, perceived in this provisional government. The Schmidt's sold the farm, migrating to Minnesota. They barely got out. It was 1923. My parents would later meet in 1942 near the conclusion of WWII.

After a courtship of less than one year, they married in Laguna Beach at the local Catholic church. Kathryn enjoyed watching the white swallows of San Juan gathering at the old Mission site. They journeyed down to the Ensenada seacoast of Mexico.

For the rest of his life, Al kept the wheelchair in the closet for his after-work rest. He didn't show it to anyone but his close family, but his back was painful after work. His job as an Executive for a government agency was demanding, working from 6am-3pm daily with the disenfranchised and unemployed workers of Watts. Many of these people were completely alienated from the system due to poverty, prejudice and lack of opportunity.

Al Downey left everyday around 5am returning around 3pm daily. He always had a ride share because he could never drive after the war. It caused him too much back pain; therefore he either walked or was in a ride share situation from age forty-two to seventy. He always took his wheelchair to work in the ride share vehicle. He remained at his place of employment for thirty-eight years. He received a gold watch for his trouble. He sold it for charity, finding it too ostentatious to wear.

He eventually taught himself how to pass the bar exam from a series of law books he had found at a local bazaar. Referring to them daily, after work, for many long hours. He memorized axioms of law to utilize them, to aid immigrants to attain work visas and eventual citizenship.

He always said he took a humdrum job for his children's sake. He said they were the apple of his eye. It was what he lived for, his children. So he kept going daily to Watts in the ghetto of Los Angeles. Later as his salary increased in his executive position, he decided to open up an office on Grand Ave. in Downtown Los Angeles, where he worked after 3pm-10pm nightly. He became a workaholic at this point. That old set of law books sure came in handy. He worked to improve on Civil Rights legislation there. When incumbent Mayor Sam Yorty ran for Mayor of Los Angeles in 1962, Al ran against him on the Democratic ticket just to oust him. He garnered around 200,000 votes which gave him more power in the legislature. Al was a real "Son of a Gun."

"Hitler had planted one million land mines in Rome alone. Pete pushed him out of the way, as the shrapnel went up Al's back. He had to be sent to Saint James infirmary for awhile. They shipped him off to the American Hospital in Paris to recuperate.

While there, he began to write screenplays in his cot about his war experiences, now totaling seventeen years as a Corporal. He penned a romantic story which became the film, "April in Paris", under a pseudonym, "Al Schwartz." Al worked for MGM as a screenwriter after the war, penning many stories.

It starred Gregory Peck, his good buddy, whom he met in Paris while on leave. Al had sent many army journals to *Le Figaro,* a leading Parisian newspaper, to print out war movements. This served to comfort the French Madames about their boy's in arms. The French people eagerly awaiting the news about their boys at the front, grab the latest *Le Figaro* as it came off the press.

Mr. Gregory Peck was an officer stationed near Rheims at that time. He spent several years in the heat of battle near the sea coast. Many of his friends were killed during "D" Day, which had sustained innumerable, heavy casualties. He later was forced to stay at the American hospital near Paris due to battle wounds. Peck was a Colonel with the U.S. forces. While resting there, he formed an alliance with certain celebrities named; William Holden, Audrey Hepburn, Ralph Gleason et al. They worked with the "Resistance" to alleviate the pressure of Hitler's Reich on the French people. It demanded about forty-five lives in show biz, in order to protect the refugees passing through. Al although confined to a wheelchair, could forge certain required documents needed for passage for children into London, to host families in New York.

He was proud to spend his days creating fake passports. Visa's and identity docs were forged in a small walkup office near the Champs Elysee.

Mr. Peck met and married Dominique a journalist, from *Le Figaro,* who he met at Sardi's. While recuperating in Paris from an open wound on his chest, their romance blossomed. Their romance became the basis for Al's script, "April in Paris". Al was impressed with their romance which tickled him. This MGM production starred Mr. Peck and Ava

Gardner. Al focused on the "joie du vivre" of his weeks while in Paris on leave.

Although in recovery from his wounds; he found Paris charming. This began to sooth his traumas from battle. He would wax poetic after gazing down the Seine, on a bridge too far from the mad scene in Berlin. These war traumas remain in him the rest of his life. It had taken away his personhood. It had taken from these soldiers, their self-respect and sense of dignity. It had treated men as if they were things rather than persons. Al felt spiritually and morally bereft. He attended Mass daily for spiritual sustenance. When he discovered Notre Dame Cathedral in Paris, he was struck by its moody beauty. This Gothic Cathedral, with its tall spires, reaching up to heaven, the interior full of colorful glass; in magenta, dark blue and green, shimmering in the light transfixed him. He felt like a new man when he passed though the majestic portals.

The carnage was incredible in London town. Bombings had obliterated thousands of buildings. The reconstruction had already begun. These British had stood up to Fascism, suffered the blows, surviving with honor. They "Kept a stiff upper lip," maintaining their dignity, on Churchill's strenuous advice.

Al always refused to describe the carnage to his family. But he was convinced that fighting Hitler's regime was the only answer! He said to his children that Americans had to protect democracy at home and abroad. It was being stomped out brutally by the Third Reich. When FDR called, he had volunteered to serve. He believed so strongly that Hitler's stomping had to be relinquished. He said, and I quote," I am going to kick that son of a bitch to hell and back!"

In order to protect millions of innocent people, destined for annihilation by this Fascist regime; Allied forces moved in under the leadership of Franklin Delano Roosevelt; Winston Churchill, General Charles De Gaulle, Willie Brandt, General Eisenhower, & General Montgomery et al. Their objective was to rescue millions from concentration camps, where they practiced death by gassing. However, it was too late for the majority of prisoners to be liberated successfully. This was a huge blow to the Allied forces. Al saw the decomposed bodies, the starvation of these people, who had become all skin and bone. Worse, Al witnessed certain Hausfraus gladly throwing these people, into open mass graves with abandon. He passed his memoirs to me, his only daughter. Al passed away in 1989, after writing speeches for politicians in his home office.

Some six million were poisoned or gassed to death by the Third Reich. People who cannot grasp the enormity of this murdered group deny it. Young people refuse to face it out of sheer disbelief. But it happened. It all happened.

Al had to relearn to walk later on, as the shrapnel made it's was to his lower spine. He learned to use a wheelchair for four long years. After many visits to the VA hospital he began to walk again. It took fifteen surgeries but it worked. When Al was sent home to the U.S. in 1942. He had to spend many hours at the V.A. learning to use a walker, then on crutches, with physical therapists aiding him, at the hospital.

His rehabilitation at the VA hospital had allowed him to dance with my mother, when he first saw her in Long Beach, at a local PX dance for returning vets. Dazzled by the woman with the long, green, emerald, satin dress and a white gardenia in her black, raven hair. He was bowled over by her innocent beauty. This small town, farm girl had finally escaped Germany's worst days. Katrina had arrived in Minnesota at age twelve, placed in the Orphanage with the Sisters of Mercy in Mankato.

They danced to Pennsylvania 4-500, a Jimmy Dorsey tune. The "Big Band Era," was in full swing. After he met Kathryn, all he wanted to do was dance his lady around, showering her with red, red roses until the day he died.

THE HAGUE

It was 1943, a year of judgment. Many Nazi war criminals had been brought before, the international court for war crimes, "The Hague Tribunal in Nuremberg," Germany.

Some had committed such horrible atrocities against the human race that they were dealt with swiftly. Otherwise war criminals were tried according to the law of international accords like "The Geneva Convention", which from 1932-1945 was dishonored by the Gestapo repeatedly. The Third Reich, for example tortured officers, in officer concentration camps. Al Downey was tortured with a cattle prod by Gestapo Agent Rickhauser, in complete defiance of the Geneva Accords. They prohibited the torture of officers when taken as POW'S. When questioned about the orphan's flight out of occupied France; he was jabbed constantly with a cattle prod below the belt. He refused for two hours to answer any questions, but eventually broke under the pain. The shame of it haunted him the rest of his life. Between this torture, combined with the pain of the shrapnel, which had dug its way into his lower spine; Al was crippled. He strongly believed that it was for life. He had lost his ability to walk for awhile. Dad often quoted Thomas Mann on this subject. He said," There is no greater love than to give up your life for a friend. "This kind of love in Catholicism is called "agape." It is a non-sexual brotherly or sisterly love, which sustains itself throughout a lifetime.

After the train to Rouen is halted midway by Gestapo agent's in transit from Berlin; the fourth regiment, took a blow, crippling the operation. Several officers were arrested for transporting kinder from Berlin with false documents. They were roughed up a the station, walked out of the endless train car to the platform.

Stan was jabbed in the stomach with the butt of the rifle. Al then proffered the guard with a cigarette and said," No need for the rough stuff boys." He opened up his coat, "Take a look at me pocket boys. I am a Corporal. My documents are inside my vest coat pocket. There are reasons for what I do. Take a look at me instructions." He then asked the guard for a light which he gave him. Lighting up a cigarette he was walked to the waiting black car. They transported a stunned Stan and Al to a Gestapo Headquarters for an interview. They were kept there many hours on the group "W" bench. Finally, after three or four hours' wait time, they were called in one by one by an impatient Corporal Rickhauser. He stomped around the room in his thigh, high black Boots, often placing his foot on the rung of the chair, to glare deeply into the eyes of the arrestees. "Why do you make me do this? I have no reason to question and officer and a gentleman like you. Make this easy for yourself. Don't dilly dally. Take a deep breath. Then tell me everything you know. This could be made easy for you. If you will only cooperate. I would not like to torture you unnecessarily. It is troublesome! Just relate what you know and I will get you a drink of wasser. Think carefully. Your fate lies in your own hands Corporal. "Then he kicks the chair with his boot leaving the room to smoke a cigarette outside the door. He chats casually with some guards. He then returns to turn on a bright bare bulb which is shone in Al's face. "Now your vill tell me everything about this or I will take stronger measures." Al pipes up "According to the Geneva Convention Accords, you cannot even question me. I choose to remain silent." "What is this? We are at war mine Herr. He places his watch on the table in front of them. Now when the hour strikes four, "Your vill relates all you know about this. If you do not, I will have to transport you to another place for internment. There is no one watching us now. It's just between us. "He pulls the chair over with his boot while he props himself up on a table looking down on Al's face. He slaps Al's face sharply with a gloved hand. He stands up once again going through some files. Al stands up from his chair "Look I have rights here! I am an Officer."

"Resume your seat. I realize Corporal Downey that you are. However, I have my orders from the Reich and must comply. I am sure in time you will understand my position. It is with pity that I must move you into our Internment Camp presently." Turning to the guard outside the door," Bring in the other prisoner" The guard escorts Mr. Stan Freiburg into the room. He stands there nervously next to Al's chair.

Corporal Rickhauser puts a gun to the temple of Freiburg's head, shooting him. Freiburg falls to the floor with a dull thud. "Take this body out. He was a filthy Jew. Take him away." Corporal Rickhauser glares at Al from his desk pointedly.

"It was my pleasure to meet you Corporal Downey." He motions to the guard posted outside the doorway. Colonel Rickhauser pushes back his chair from the desk, throwing his file on it. He then places his arms akimbo behind him stretching.

Al is escorted down the hallway in handcuffs by two, black helmeted guards. He is placed roughly, inside a white van. It travels the dirt roads for many miles outside Rouen. Al can glance at the Cathedral passing with its Gothic, rose-colored, stained glass windows, which dance in the light. They are passing through Rouen. He makes a silent prayer.

Al knows why he defended those stray kids; that these transported children have been marked for death by the Reich. It is only due to their skin color, their religion beliefs. It was all part of Hitler's plan to 'purify' his country. In fact, Hitler knows at that point that he will lose the war. The Allies have encircled him from Russia to France, Spain, Austria.

Hitler, in his diseased logic has decided to eliminate all the children, who were non-white, Aryan, Germans.

This concentration camp is located on the border of Rheims, France and Anschutz, Germany. He is quartered there for six months. These officers make many escape plans, continually trying to fool the Gestapo with tunneling out. They use spades and hoes to dig for hours and hours. The dirt is acquired from the yard where they hoe a vegetable garden daily. They make certain it never sprouts, taking dirt samples in canvas bags inserted in their pants into the yard. It is dispersed from the tunnel dirt which they remove fortuitously. These determined men ferreted out a portion of dirt, to expand into an active tunnel for evacuation purposes. It seemed interminable, but the Allies check the radio, which they somehow smuggle into the camp to their barracks. Al checks the radio for news every day, his head glued to its side. It means everything to these men to know the Allies are overturning this Fascism. There is hope on the horizon. FDR's voice tells them that 'Help is finally on the way from the U.S." The indomitable French finally overturns the Nazi incursion into their territory, by sheer force of will.

The French Army eventually liberates them all. They escape to Free France under the command of General Charles De Gaulle. Six thousand officers are liberated in one afternoon, formerly held as POW'S, under Corporal Anaheim. He is a Franco-German officer, who speaks fluent German.

Man are they glad to see De Gaulle! He wears his dress blues for the occasion out of due respect for these officers, most of whom were captured outside Berlin in the hedges, along the outlying roads.

After all was said and done after the Final Liberation; Hermann Goering, a noted physician, under the Nazi regime, receives thirty-three years. This was the maximum sentence allocated to war criminals, for crimes against humanity. His notorious experimentation with eye color on incarcerated concentration camp victims, made him one of the most notorious outlaws in history. It led many to perceive his misuse of medical knowledge was solely for diabolical purposes. His continuous experimentation on the Yaqui Indians in Venezuela along with Dr. Josef Mengele's pigmentation experiments in Buenos Aires, left behind numerous personal notebooks. They were penned with a quill in the blood of these Indians. Known for an aversion to any other eye color but blue; he annotated innumerable attempts to change their eye color, to suit his Aryan philosophy. Today in Argentina, it is still evidenced. These ghoulish displays of Nazi arrogance with innumerable tribe's people, who have patches of skin discoloration, eye discoloration or blinded. Several Nazi physicians traveled to Buenos Aires to escape incarceration there by 'The Hague Tribunal." It has tried many war criminals after the close of WWII. It is considered the world's governing court on war crimes. The goal of all these are crimes against humanity was of course, the physical embodiment of the Aryan philosophy. This continuous effort to anglicize all Indians was grotesque and disproportionate to the size of Hitler's regime.

In an all-white world, of pure Aryan features, with no variation at all, a person of Nazi beliefs would live happily. This conception of genetics was the goal of Hitler's Reich Dom. It was attempted for over thirty-three years particularly in Dresden, Germany. This seething hatred under the surface of these men bubbled over during this period.

ATTACHE

D r. Josef Mengele, a noted Nazi physician, had been incarcerated for thirteen years, after the war. He made his escape to Argentina in the latter part of the 1920's. He remained there many more years filling notebooks in blood red ink with his bizarre theories and rhetoric. Josef Mengele dreamed of a world without any variation of skin tone, appearance or facial characteristics, where clones reigned supreme. It is interesting to note that in Hollywood cloning is out of hand. Stand-Ins will literally change their facial appearance to substitute for famous actors. It takes a special person to lose their own identity in order to stand in for an actor. This eerie behavior is s harbinger of the 1930's Nazi era. A sad, dismal, reminder of the quality of life during WWII. Why would others mimic a strangers' identity in this Cult of Personality? It's an empty guise to fool others.

Dr. Mengele sought a world without browns, and Indians, a world of the so-called perfect Aryan features, espoused in Hitlerian philosophy. He went to great lengths to achieve his ends. He often utilized syringes on his patients, praising the miraculous results.

Mengele was especially cruel to women, denying them menopause in certain cases, while forcing them to reproduce to his satisfaction, or conversely denying them any means of reproductive freedom through forced abortions, particularly on Jewesses. His cruelty was so legendary in Germany, in Dresden in particular, that Jews would avoid visitations there for decades in fear of being captured, sliced open while experimented on by Gestapo troops. The Gestapo was fascinated by his ghoulish findings which he would present in Berlin at private meetings there with der Further.

Dr. Harry Abrams, acted as his personal attaché. He proudly carried his dossiers, and other briefs. Dr. Harry Abrams was so entranced by his position, he carried Mengele's keys religiously. He also, as a young doctor himself, carried out innumerable experiments on Jewish civilians. They usually resulted in the gassing of up to sixty thousand Jews, at one time, before lunch. Mengele said that it "Improved his appetite".

Mengele's idea of a good time was to munch on the innards of the Jewish women, sometimes, to scare away flimsy recruits, who he saw as unworthy for this kind of work. It usually resulted in droves of them leaving the room, belching. He also enjoyed cleansing his teeth with Jewish bones in full view of his troops. His appetite was so peculiar; he refused Sherry at 3pm and insisted on a Pauli's girl with a portion of Jewish intestines. He was already seen by many as mad. Mengele had no sex life whatsoever, preferring to write copies notes in the evening. He had no lovers, friends or amigos at all, preferring to isolate himself in his bedchamber with a chamber pot on his bed to keep him warm. When that didn't work he retired to a warmer climate, Buenos Aires. He was considered Hitler's right hand man. He was a self-contained man with no scruples whatsoever.

He thought nothing of what he did, and was even proud of it. He favored a good cigar to any dame in town, puffing on it for hours with a curious grin. Years passed before he was ever caught. He had hidden all his gruesome findings in a bunker North of the city of Leipzig. He often went their secretly at night to bury his notations under this bunker, for Hitler to pursue in the morning with his coffee, which he usually poured into the street gutters of Berlin.

Mengele's' idea of a good time was a game of pinochle. A terribly, dull man, he never acquired comradeship. He was not liked. He is often referred to as the Mad Doctor of Dresden. He frequently assaulted women to "Test their mettle" and threw them down on the floor, frequently stomping on their entrails with mad glee in full view of Gestapo agents. He hated all things feminine. When he died no one came to the funeral. Frederick Clopped secretly wanted an escape hatch in East Berlin, 1923. He searched far and wide for an answer. He found the answer in Cracow when he met and fell in love with Gretchen Holst in the dance hall located in the center of town. As he spied her with her blond-braided, shiny, waxen braids dancing in circles, he was enthralled. She wore a starched, white blouson with embroidered suspenders. She was so merry with a beautiful smile, that he was instantly smitten. After a few rounds of Pauli's girl; he worked up the courage to ask this beauty to dance. She accepted the invitation with a smile from ear to ear. He was a handsome man with a deceptively, innocent expression on his face.

Before long they were engaged to be married in Cracow, near a cathedral of her mother's choosing. This was well before the restrictions were placed on worship by the Gestapo in Germany. People still milled around the churches as a social center.

Frederick noticed the changes soon in about one year's time, when church doors became bolted shut. Placards displayed a new order on them," Exeunt". No entreat remained for seven years onevery church door throughout the nation of Germany. Was the Gestapo afraid of the spiritual? Why?

"THE ELIMINATOR"

G retchen is a loyal, cheerful wife for years. Suddenly in 1935 the Gestapo raids their home in the middle of the night.

She is so unaware of their cruelty, that she trusts them to treat her with respect. She is thrown to the sofa hastily. She had run to her door thinking it was her Frederick. They maul her cruelly raising her skirts, mocking her. She is so afraid that he is pregnant she cries for months. Frederick can not console her.

Many months pass. Later after midnight, jeeps roam the city, full of Gestapo personnel often three sheets to the wind, looping in circles around the main boulevards of Cracow.

Frederick has to tell her that he has lost his sight and is nearly blind. It is a congenital defect that begins to blind him at twenty. He feels that he will not be able to protect her enough. He has to leave her every day crying. She can't understand that he must go to work, albeit with the German army she detests.

He worries for his Gretchen. She has changed so much since the attack. They never reported it because the Gestapo were in charge. It would mean their execution. Gretchen has been seen by these men outside, tending her garden regularly and going to market. They will whistle and hoot at her loudly on the streets.

However, when they raid her, they made sure her husband was away at his night job, and torment the girl to tears. After this experience she refuses to have sexual intercourse again. She closes down completely, doubting her attractiveness. She loses all desire. They continue to haunt her. On the streets they taunt, her calling her every name they devise spitting at her.

Gretchen is so lovely that he could never leave her. He has made a vow which he sees as his honor. In order to survive this Gestapo encroachment, and to blend in with the insidious Nazi Regime; Frederick decides to become a spy, an insider for the underground movement.

After his training in Cracow, he is given a fake badge to sport. He wears a black leather coat past his knees, black polished shoes with black socks. He approaches many people in the street asking questions, flashing a badge that is silver, carried in a navy-blue plastic holder. Many people believe that he is an important official, never to be contradicted or questioned himself.

He has an aura of authority which tricks most town folk. He enjoys lording it over others. It gives him back the power he had lost when his Gretchen was attacked so fiercely. In fact, he fakes ii most of the time. In order to pass, for part of the regime of Heinrich Himmler; he dons their uniform.

Himmler is an erudite man, about six feet tall, elegant, intelligent almost a brainier. Frederick has the notion that he can survive the war, if he plays along with these Gestapo. He now views them as his opposition due to the rape of his wife. And play he does.

He utilizes many others to his advantage; following them continually, telling them stories. These lies mask his own intentions. It works beautifully because he is never caught while doing his duties. His job is to interrogate the masses under the Gestapo Regime who have offended Herr Hitler. He knows what the Gestapo are beginning to do. They gas numerous gypsies in a camp daily, never reporting any of it to anyone.

After awhile Mr. Kluppen becomes notorious in the bars for his lackadaisical treatment of the frauleins, frequently looking up their skirts with chagrin. He is so handsome they often fall for his act. However, after a few minutes they can see that he is definitely not marriage material.

Girls can sense the Gestapo has strenuous designs on them. These designs often make them their regular stop for sexual encounters wanted or not. These frauleins cannot say no. Their mothers are even smacked across the face with gloves, if they refuse these men. If the girls are Juden, they were simply taken from their homes, then executed either in the street or in camps. Many girls simply react by ignoring these come-ons. This only works for a while. What these men desired they act on without mercy. Thousands of young girls are placed in camps, for their refusal to either work there or are incarcerated. The keys are thrown away. However, one girl named Gretchen is so hot to trot, that she even surpasses all of his expectations.

He is so surprised when she volunteers to put out; sitting on his lap for an hour. He is intimidated by her aggressive mode.

She is a small, blonde girl with verve. She is never allowed to be alone, or to go to nightclubs. Her father beats he down so flatly, that she has no more feeling for him or any other man, for the remainder of her existence. Her life will be short due to her religion. She has run away to join the club crowd. She need thrills. These boys in makeup and pasty-faced, cream are so effeminate they appeal to her. She has some fragile connection to them. They have rejected the superhuman cruelty of the others in the Party. However, it never showed on her small, piquant face which is always in a pinched expression above her intense brown eyes.

She is in constant ecstasy because she bounces on Frederick like a rubber ball for hours jumping up and don on his lap. He can see that she needs absolute control over him. He lets her. She has the most open, aggressive attitude that he has seen in years. Sarah treats Frederic like a Butterfingers bar. To her the wrapper is simply a disposable item for her insatiable appetites. She would idly stare at the ceiling watching a spider cross over it, then gaze at her fingernail polish with disdain.

He is only a moment of pleasure, easily cast aside. At first he is struck by her indifference. Later realizing that she really is truly indifferent to him; it hardens his heart even more. He pursues this little girl for years for sexual pleasure; escorting her all over town on weekend trips to vari-ous resorts. But he cannot even skim over her smooth exterior. She never falls in love with him, viewing him as an amusing boy-toy.

When asked about him, she denies ever knowing him, with a scowl. It is a gross embarrassment for a Jew to be seen with these Angles in clubs. Gretchen never feels anything after sex but what someone would feel after a delicious dessert. She has advanced to the level of detachment, known to few female's ins society. She is accepted as a "tough broad" with little demands for affection, from her consorts, which she conquers frequently. Other girls are amazed at her detached air.

Frederick becomes her go-to sex object. He is so handsome he is like eye candy to her. Gretchen later decides to steal his purse, spending five thousand dollars per day, on silly sex toys for fun times. She has a predilection for oral sex which is notorious. She often tucks little gifts in her décolleté for fun asking a Gestapo agent to pull them out of her brassiere with his teeth. As she seduces the Germans officer she becomes known as "Lolita." She has acquired several beautiful diamond necklaces which she keeps to herself, often using them to entice her lovers, whom she will tangle with only for money. She recognizes Frederick's love of glitter and gold.

At one point she handcuffs Frederick to his bed, leaving him there alone for hours. She goes gallivanting throughout the city stealing furs, and jewelry from local homes. She decides to pin the crimes on him. She has taken his fingerprints from a glass of Courvoisier. Lolita piles up furs and jewels next to the bed, grinning at him. She finally unlocks the cuffs around 4am.She is now dripping in ermine and pearls with diamond bracelets up to her elbow from these nightly sojourns. Her life is now a game of acquisition, sloth, and lux living?

Gretchen is a true "Existentialist", living only for the moment of thrills and spills. To her there so no future at all! Like Albert Camus, she sees the end of their world coming around every corner. She never acknowledges anything beyond her immediate thrills.

At first Frederick found her fun and engaging, an adorable toy.

However, like all toys, he tires of this little broken rag-a- muffin, throwing her into his pile in the corner. He attracts so many babes it is gluttonous. For Frederick there is no end to the adoration of beauties.

But to him, his lovely wife, remains by far so unique, he adores her. Until she takes her own life.

He is driving his sedan on his way to work as usual, near them cottage. She insists on jumping in front of the wheel of the car. She deliberately blocks his moving vehicle. Frederick can not brake fast enough to stop. She lays there on the ground, motionless for minutes. He tries to carry her to help, but finds no helpers in these desolate streets. So he walks and walks, carrying her for several blocks.

No one comes to his assistance. It is a dark, lonely night far from the madding crowd. He has to lay her to rest himself after washing her delicate face lovingly, kissing her forehead. She has given up on life itself. He buries her in the park. No one ever notices them. After this incident, he becomes a hardened soul, oblivious to deep emotion. He decides to live in the hinterlands of the region. He boards up their whitewashed, cottage in Cracow. For a time, no longer engaged in sex with anyone, considering them dirt under his feet. He begins to curse her under his breath. Later he goes back to the nightclubs to play with the frailties. They are just used to fulfill momentary needs, then disposed of like Kleenex.

Frederick goes searching for laborers to fulfill work orders given to him by a commandant, whom he has encountered in Warsaw. He manages to round up over five hundred men daily for labor. Many have rags wrapped around their feet for shoes, and gloves without fingers. They stand in the cold, bitter morning at 5am waiting, always waiting for a command ate to hire them. After they are worked for ten to twelve hours, he will shoot one. It is an example to the others not to argue with him or make trouble. He becomes known as a fierce companion to the Gestapo. They respect his deliberate malice, honoring his code of violence. Frederick Clopped has acquired a reputation for merciless elimination of those he dubs his inferiors. Those who disappoint him are snuffed out. It is part and parcel of his Aryan philosophy.

He is so notorious the laborers called him, "The Eliminator". In five years, he has a few," pesetas" but is unhappy with his lot in life. He soon acquires another companion, by kidnapping a gracious British lady from a filling station nearby. She is seated in her car waiting for her lover, when he notices her smile. He drags her out of the model "T ". He throws her into his own truck gruffly. After a few minutes he tells her," You will have a better time with me!" bluntly slamming the truck door shut. Naturally, she cried bitter tears at his abduction.

He drives her through miles of desolate roads to an abandoned shack where he rapes her. She is so shocked she buckles over like a small, new-born child. He refuses to listen to her pleas, slapping her frequently until she complies with him. He will not let go. This British visitor becomes his companion for years. She is as white as white could be, in keeping with his philosophy. She has black, penetrating eyes. When she tries to escape he dislocates her shoulder several times. No one notices or helps this kidnap victim. It is so commonplace in Warsaw during this war. She cannot go back to England fearing that he will kill her sisters there. She has three, who were unawares of this incident. He sequesters her in a small whitewashed cottage again, as if she was a replacement. If her family aided her, he would have to eliminate them. That is his code. The Nazi code that he has embraced. She is a British newscaster for the BBC in London.

If she would have only guessed his intentions at the gas station outside Warsaw; then she would never have been so gracious him. She wants to kick herself. She has no way home to England again. She only sees a handsome man in him but truly surly. He has the quality of an actor hell-bent on destruction.

To her this abduction is permanent. Due to her many attempts to leave, which are foiled, she slowly became resigned to her fate. He will rant, rave and stalk, repeatedly tracking her throughout the city of Berlin. He acts the wolverine searching for her. Frederick is a night crawler, only squirming after 2am. She finds a way to avoid his search-lights which he strategically places on the front of his black sedan. He uses them to spot a fawn startled by his glaring, insistent spotlights.

This BBC journalist is never the same. She has lost all contact with her family in Ireland and England. He cuts off her phone lines using a teletype machine to communicate with the gestapo. She has to live with the permanent separation, the loss of her three daughters in Ireland, permanently. She resorts to drinking decanters of Brandy as a painkiller.

Frederick needs her constant attention at all times. His need was so great, he never imagines her deep pain. He is truly a blind man. After some months of this forced relationship, she accustoms herself to being whipped with a cat of nine tails constantly. The cuts are so bad that she has to develop her own salve. No one hears her moans or cries for help. He has kept her in a cottage remote from the city. She thinks that she must represent to him a symbol of the Allies; a reason to hate. This refined, British lady has one request of him, that he buy her only the finest tea and jam for her biscuits.

She has left behind all she loved, to be his consort, knowing that he will never survive this war without her companionship, albeit forced.

WESTERN UNION

A l receives a Western Union telegram from General Eisenhower. Al is intent on "seizing the day" a favorite quote of his. He feels that he has a commander's grip on his desk agenda. Stashing a scrap of paper into his raincoat pocket, he leaves his desk.

Then suddenly heads out into a Rouen rainstorm to locate the private phone booth, he grabs his vectored hat. Secrecy is vital at this juncture.

His favorite secretary Mabel has previously made a vital appointment with General Eisenhower "Ike", concerning an issue of paramount importance to Al. The fighting Third regiment was guided by General Patton himself. Ike has generated this operation, supplying funding under an FDR Bill passed in 1936, through the Senate funding to develop maneuvers. After some crucial strategy, an escape hatch is launched, utilizing the convents around El Vatican City, as well as local family cottages near Centro. This occurs, after a needed resolution was implemented immediately in order to proceed. Dashing into the stormy phone booth; he clutches the phone. Anxiously he calls headquarters in London. It's so cold, Al's raincoat is pulled up over his ears.

The General has been called away. Dripping, he exits the phone booth, heaving a deep sigh, returning to his own offices in Rheims. Two hours later, a recalcitrant secretary has cancelled the appointment due to an imminent crisis called in by General Eisenhower. Al's spirit plummets.

Without an okay, how can he proceed with this operation? Throughout his tour of Mammal, he had witnessed nothing but thousands of wandering children amongst the marble and stone rubble of

Roma. They forage for food through remains and debris, chomping on old Italian bread loaves, drinking sewer water. These children are either orphaned or dispossessed of their homes and families. He and his men prefer to proffer chocolate bars and pantyhose, which the children and teens eagerly sell for fresh loaves from the bakery. Al knows that they are all cannon fodder on the street.

From his soggy tent near the front of Palermo base camp; he has conceived a Master Plan to airlift, and relocate these orphans through unoccupied France, to London Airport, England to America. Why not include his cousins; U.S. Airman Ode Smith and ACE fighter pilot, Myron Schmidt, who is stationed in Paris?

Their homes and families gone, these street urchins have little time left. Al has witnessed first-hand, an angry commandant eliminating these street children at close range with shots to the head, in full view of the Italian peasants in the village. The people there secretly hate the Reich, but due to Mussolini's secret forged agreements, they will play along to survive the war. Some in the underground witness these atrocities, while plotting to overthrow the interlopers in their nation.

The empty, brown eyes of these children, their bodies contorted in pain, have moved Al so much. He has teletyped Rome Headquarters, after drafting several memos which were sent from Patton's offices in Rouen, France. "Save these children now! before the seven percent solution becomes the goal here." In August 1935, Hitler's madness includes eliminating all children of color from this planet by genocide, who do not conform to his Aryan stereotype of perfection. This includes; all Jew, Gypsies, Latinos, Africans, Moslems, the mentally retarded, and other challenged children, not considered "perfect," according to their ethos.

These imminent teletypes are received promptly. General Eisenhower is in the process of considering the implementation of a huge operation, which is now underway. Al cannot fathom the extent of it throughout Western Europe.

FDR, the Commander in Chief is so moved by these requests for Eisenhower; he has authorized a bill through Congress and the Senate immediately to squelch this infamy. A clean-up campaign is now underfoot. Now thanks to American compassion, these children in rag-a-muffin clothes have a way out. Operation Blackfoot is now granted to the 3rd and 4th Regiment whenever feasible, due to their furious engagement with the enemy. Thrilled, Al picks up the teletype in Patton's office. His job as a clerk is to report troop movements. He has worked near Beirut for seventeen years there. He practically jumps for joy upon receipt of orders!

This is a way to redeem these men from guilt and pain associated with this brutal war. They now can show that they are bound and intent on accomplishing something good, once and for all. The plan is approved by Ike to smuggle and air lift the majority of these children out "by any means necessary," through France and England.

While on leave in Montpelier, Al thinks that it is strategic to contact his first cousin, Myron Schmidt. He is an ACE flyer stationed nearby near Paris, what is now Charles de Gaulle Airport. Myron is a proud German-American émigré from the Lichtenstein area.

Myron hails from Minnesota, one of eleven children on a small German farm near Mankato. Myron has assumed the rank of U.S. Airman with ease. His aeronautical skills are quite remarkable. He is a sensational flying ACE. He has climbed the ranks in France to Colonel, to run dangerous reconnaissance missions, under General De Gaulle in keeping with FDR's joint agreements. Al and Myron Schmidt have planned to meet on the airfield around 1500 hours.

Al spots Myron's jet pull up on the runway. He is surprised to see Myron's smiling face in the cockpit waving at him. The cockpit opens up. "Hop on in, Al!". "I'll be glad to take you for a spin." Unaware of Myron's humor, he willingly boards the cockpit. The wing span on this baby is about thirty feet. Myron hands him a helmet smiling. The plane is cranked up by a mechanic, at the exterior, spinning the lever around and around. Al has no idea what he is in for yet. Speedily, Myron heads for the bright blue skies, willy-nilly.

They spin upside down, Myron bucking it up, as he flips this baby over. The plane is making loop de loops at a 360-degree curl, tearing through the skies with an ACE at the wheel. Al does all he can to hold his cookies. There's another spin with a free fall, then a sudden drop. Al's mind is boggled. Myron is showing off like an ACE trickster.

For a free thrill ride, it costs Al his lunch, but unswerved he holds his barf bag in place. Myron does not look back, making another 360-degree spin. Finally, Al pounds on the window in front of him. "Okay Myron, no more, no more. That will do." Myron has cheerfully performed his aeronautical tricks with ease, never thinking about this ground warrior. "Enough already, old man." "Okay Al, but I thought you wanted a demo?" "Yeah, I got the picture. You're the ACE!" staring at his wobbly legs.

Myron swoops this plane down in short order, opening up the cockpit. Myron stands up to regard Al, who sheepishly remains in his seat. His hands are holding onto the sides of the interior, clutching. "Are we there yet? "he glances up with trusting eyes at Myron.

"Well I guess I was showing off; but I wanted you to see what this baby could do". "Hope you survived the demonstration!" Myron. "Yes, but I am a trifle wobbly." Finally, Al stands up, exiting the cockpit. On the ground he takes his dress blue hat, twirling it around in his hand slowly, searching for words. 'What I really wanted to talk to you about was orders from Headquarters. "Well if we're going to get serious; let's head for the mess hall." Al sheepishly, "I think I'll just have coffee thanks."

TOW HEADED GIRL

As Avril Smith walks into the Embassy Regal Hotel, in beautiful, downtown Saint Paul; everyone can see that he is a handsome, elegant and brilliant politician. His black hair is slicked back to show off his flashing blue eyes. He is dressed in a vested suitcoat with watch and chain at hand. He hails from Mankato, Minnesota. He has cut his teeth on law books for several years prior to his law school application entrance exam. It propelled him through law school to the seat in Congress in 1945 to 1975.

Mr. Smith has his little tow headed daughter Ellen in hand. She, in a yellow, dirndl dress with her hair slapped down just so with Vaseline, is balking audibly. It is her twelve-year-old habit to yank out every gossamer strand of her hair, pluckily in the presence of his quests. It often confuses this widower, who has lost his beautiful wife, when his daughter was born. Ellen is so wrapped up in herself, she cannot relate to others at all.

She frequently curses like a sailor loudly, blurting out such morbid obscenities, people will stare at them everywhere. At "terrible two", she is like a little devil, tossing matches at her father suits, to ruin his clothes. She even sets a pile of her mother's clothes alight in the middle of the living room. It causes such a storm of confusion; Avril wraps his suit coat around his arm, trying to not only douse the fire but pulls his infant daughter to safety.

Ellen then gets back at her father by having sex with a neighbor boy, voluntarily out of curiosity. After word got out about the disrobing little miss; the neighbor boys then began to use her, mocking her behind her back. Avril has to step in constantly, taking time off his work. He has to take this nonsequiter to every clinician and therapist in town. Luckily this politician has the love and support of the pubic. Now Ellen has also learned not to screech, scream and curse in public places. It took so many arduous hours of work to change her way of being. In special needs classes near Saint Paul, Mr. Avril Smith has his hands full with his only child.

At age twelve, of course, she is pregnant, having had sex with four of the neighbor's boys in a country shed at once. To them it is just a good time. She has no boundaries to her nature, no self-respect at all. To her it is just nothing to her, to entertain these neighbors with her body.

Naturally, her dad is beside himself with worry. She is the talk of the small town of Mankato. Frequently she walks around in various stages of undress, hitchhiking rides. Avril is certain some stranger will beat or kill her if she persists in this behavior. It is so hard to stop her.

He confines her, on the physician's advice, to a home for special needs children near Mankato. Ellen hates it, but it keeps her alive and kicking.

Mr. Avril Smith decides to run for Congress, determined as part of his platform, to help the severely mentally ill persons in Minnesota with new bills, fresh ideas.

He wins. He serves in Congress twelve years. His death is mysterious. Several years go by his little family is growing. His daughter is still attending special classes. Averill is found in a pool of blood outside Mankato, near a creek. His little daughter has disappeared off the face of this earth without a trace. She is never located again. The family fears kidnapping of this frightened child.

Chow Down

It is a beautiful, Midwestern, Sunday afternoon. Kathryn and Evelyn have the children stashed in the back of the old Chevy, going to Sunday supper at Ode Smith's ranch at 3pm. They are expecting a feast because eleven of the children of Margaret Smith are coming for this reunion. Katy is dressed in her very best brown, paisley patterned dress, with a diamond brooch at the side like. The twirling skirt reminds Marie of dancing. She smells like a bowl of gardenias in bloom.

When Katy and Evelyn arrive there, they are warmly greeted and immediately ushered into a sun porch, at a huge oak table in the round. On the table are white, starched, linen cloths, with napkins presented amongst high, family style, bowls of fresh sweet corn, scrumptious biscuits dripping in butter, green string beans in bacon drippings, a huge, spiral, honey ham, farm raised fried chicken, mashed potatoes, with homemade apricot jam. But first grace.

They all bow their heads collectively as Ode leads a small thankful prayer for their bounty from their farm.

As huge ceramic bowls are cheerfully passed country style around the table, Ode sees the two city kids from Los Angeles regarding this enormous German family. "Have some homemade raspberry jam," as he slaps a huge spoonful onto David's plate. David is miffed at the service, the country manners. "These guys are nothing but old fogies, country bumpkins", he smirks at Maria, who giggles into her napkin. He is brought up formally with sophisticated ways in LA, unused to these corn chomping, Midwesterners. He glares at Ode. Dave is twelve and full of beans himself. Maria is so thrilled to have homemade anything; she gobbles up the biscuits in jam and butter with glee. At ten years of age she has a pageboy haircut, a frilly, yellow dress with a peter pan collar. Katy is proud to show off her two brilliant children to her uncles and aunts. While they are dining, Dave sneaks off to investigate the house entirely. He pokes his nose into medicine cabinets and bedrooms. Katy has to pull him out of one of the bedrooms. Maria is getting bored too; kicking her legs under the table and leaning on her hand while gazing about the room. "We'll leave in awhile dear," Katy gently reminded her. The conversation gets more animated over dessert. A huge, peach pie is introduced as well as apple and cherry, with fresh homemade whipping cream, laced with cinnamon. These delicious pies are passed around with fresh, hot coffee cups.

As they eat and happily talk; Maria and David spy a strange little girl across the table with her hand in her father's pocket. She is a tow headed, mouthy, blue-eyed, girl suddenly cursing a blue streak at Avril.

She refuses to even look at others focusing only on her father. "Did you bring me a present? "she asks him. She insists on a gift loudly, embarrassed. She looks about twelve. To the children, she is so standoffish, that they continue to ignore her. Suddenly she blurts out a steady stream of invective at her father, who stands by her in a gray, seersucker suit, vest, watch and chain. He is so used to it he's almost nonreactive.

Katy leans over whispering. "You must be shocked. She acts abnormally, often screaming and fighting her dad. "As David rolls his eyes to heaven. He gazes lovingly at his mom saying "Okay we get it". Maria glares at Kathryn. "When you are older you will understand." "Oh you always say that and I never understand anything! "Maria blurts out, kicking the floor.

Maria has been adopted at three and one half from Louisiana. She is brought up around deep Southern language and has a distinct drawl, which attracts attention. Her father, Al says that she will never lose her drawl. Al told her that it will only hold her back in society. So Maria tries to lose her drawl constantly and self-consciously, thinking herself inferior to Southern Californians from day one.

Now in Minnesota, they thought these country bumpkins are hu-morous, attempting to stifle their laughter continually.

Their father, Al has been brought up in a wealthy, Irish home in Cork, Ireland as well as Indiana. They always have sherry before dinner; the men with cigars. Dad was always in his smoking jacket, then they retired to the dinner table for a full three course meal daily. The dinner bell is always rung precisely at 3pm. Orderves are sorely missed unless served first in the living room. Plates of crudité, salads are served in a Lazy Susan as a discussion takes place before dinner.

Conversation, usually politically inclined, permeates this home. Al has even run for Mayor of Los Angeles against Mayor, Sam Yorty, the perennial incumbent. Yorty is controlled by so many gangsters it's pa-thetic. Al Downey garners 20% of the vote Downtown Los Angeles. This gives him a political power base in the Senate in Sacramento, to negotiate bills. Later he moves up to the Congress for the twenty-fifth Congressional District, in Washington D.C. by taking the place of an absentee Congressman, for two years, as a Proxy on the explicit advice of Sargent Shriver. He is listed five times in the Congressional Record for his work in Congress. Al uses this power base to push Civil Rights Bills through the Senate.

Manners are emphasized at all times in their home. Everything here is strange and new. The women seem coarse, ill-mannered and vulgar, in cotton shifts, no makeup or perfume. It puzzles the young teenagers.

But as plates of food are whizzing around the bend like wildfire, everyone is well stuffed by end of day. Even in this small village, the conversation turns to politics, as Avril is asked his opinions by Ode and others. They admire his brilliant mind; his experiences in Congress is impressive. His word is gold to them.

The twelve German-American children all have made a success in farming, when they relocate from Alsace Lorraine just after the Reichdom incursion into the countryside. Near Alsace, the jeeps filled up with Brownshirts. They have raided the farms, stolen buckets of produce readily, without compunction.

These young men, gamely loaded it into their squad cars. Yelling

curses at elders in the name of the Reich; they fully expected farmers
to feed them freely. It was to be the greatest Depression Germany had
ever seen. These occurrences were so frequent; Harry Schmidt begins to
prepare more and more buckets of grain, produce, and corn for these
hoodlums to raid, as they pass through their countryside in raiding
parties frequently.

Armed with Brown shirts, swastikas burned into her forearms, carrying little black books in their rear pockets, these Hitler Youth, took
no prisoners. They tell the local farmers that they frequently shooting
pistols into the air, in a show of force. Their crudeness is becoming
common place.

Harry Schmidt knew it is getting about time to pull up roots,
leaving his beloved country for America. As Harry heard in the village
nearby, the plans of these men to purify Germany of Jews, gypsies and
the like. As a God fearing reverent Catholic, he realizes now that their
entire clan of Smiths would soon be in danger in this Godless society
of brutes as well.

It becomes imminent to plan stealthily, bundling off twelve entire
siblings to America before the curtain comes down strongly, sharply.
They could not exit this madness. The burgeoning, fascistic government
is slowly turning with the Weimar Republic to an even greater fascism,
with new perceived charismatic leadership. This regime plots the destruction of all perceived enemies of the state. It is in the wind. Time to
escape the blackness to follow.

It's a puzzle why anyone in his right mind would remain in this
cursed society, as dozens of their fellow neighbors disappear or are hauled
away for minor offenses as stipulated by the new Republic.

Ode Schmidt, one of the twelve Schmidt's, is a fighter ACE for
the U.S. stationed near Calais for five years. Eventually he will attain
a Silver Star. He later returns to Saint Paul, Minnesota to live out his
life on a ranch, as he had original dreamed. Mr. Ode Schmidt, due to a
backlash against Germans, is forced to change his name to Ode Smith.
All German citizenry in Minnesota experienced heavy prejudice after
the war.

All the Schmidt's changed their names, all forty of them, to avoid needless persecution, taunts, and sideways glances. In 1948, a proud clan of Germans had Anglicized their names in toto to protect their futures, in the land they fought bravely to protect from fascism.

RECONNASSAISANCE

I t's 1938, as Ode Schmidt steps out of his cockpit in the blustery rain-storm over Paris. He tilts his face up towards the drizzle, refreshing and clean. Ode has been stationed near the Gare D'Orsay for over three years. His missions become only reconnaissance over Southern Germany during the height of the war. As he saunters along long legged, and re-laxed to the command post headquarters; he is feeling his oats.

After this last hair raising mission, he is not surprised to hear from Corporal Al Downey by teletype from Rouen. Al communicates the new mission," Operation Blackfoot" to take place shortly. He advises Ode, that they could use his talents as a flyboy to circumvent the Panzers in the air, by confusing them; as airlifted convoys of personnel fly into occupied territory. It is 1936. The air swarms with Panzers, like crows flying low over the Black Forest.

Delighted to hear from Corporal Downey; he sends a communique to consent to any and all missions related to this operation. Al is thrilled to have several ACE pilots at his disposal for a difficult task ahead. It is now 1400 hours. News spreads quickly throughout the encampment of Rouen that airlifting, as well as ground troops, will be utilized to move thousands of children out of occupied areas. They are moving them into Allied regions under strict supervision. This mission entails the forgery of many new documents to afford them escape routes through occupied areas into Switzerland, unoccupied France, England and the United States. Replacement clothing is required for all the children. Al thinks long and hard about how to achieve all this. Suddenly it occurs to him to visit the Vatican. As he strides along the marbled pavements of the portico area; he glances to the right of Saint Peter's Basilica. He knocks on some doors. A small Italian nun comes to the door. He is in his dress blues, so is welcomed inside the lobby area. His father has taught him long ago in Ireland, when in trouble ask the Sisters of the Immaculate Heart for help.

Weeks later these sisters would be clothing, feeding and hiding many children. They themselves, become the forgers for the regiment. To avoid suspicion from Nazi visitors and questions; they no longer communicate with the "Fighting Third." Soldiers will simply send the children to them insisting they walk, not run to the door. The transformation is now in place. These children will assume new identities easily, hand-me-downs that have been refurbished to suit their needs. Dozens at a time will visit the sisters, usually at day break, before the German troops are awakened. They slip right through their hands. The German jeeps frequently stop at the Vatican. One commandant visits every Sunday, removing his black leather gloves slowly.

He wears a black, visored hat striding the length and breadth of the portico. Now entering a great hallway with fifty-foot ceilings, he admires the frescoes in pastel colors up above. He is tilting his head up like an eager child. As he passes by the Swiss Guard posts, he nods to the guards at times. He is not looking for anything in particular. Hitler has sent him there to acquiesce treasures.

Otto Kleinfelder has been at this post for several years, while occupied Italy's Mussolini makes secret plans to storm the Vatican. Hitler is planning to steal all of its treasures. This plan is never executed because the Italian troops simply will not permit it. Hitler has already sacked the Louvre in Paris. Many of those treasures have been hidden away by the French underground successfully. However, many are absconded to Berlin to appeal to Hitler's sensibilities. He chooses particular works, which stress the Aryan mindset, featuring Aryan models of blonde femininity, and muscle bound, blonde, Trojan males as symbols of white purity. These works are then shown at the Chancellery, regularly to appeal to the Gestapo, complete with dinner parties, orderves trays and champagne on Saturday nights.

Gestapo agents party there, regularly, celebrating their booty. A great many art objects are sacked all over Europe. Then they are either bestowed to Nazis as prizes for heroism, or sold on the black market later. The museum collections are permanently dispersed all over occupied territories.

Pablo Picasso, the famed Spaniard painter, heralded as the greatest of the 20th century by many critics, heard of this forced seizure of artwork. He decides with the help of the French underground, to quickly hide many of his works in a farmhouse in Arles. This works for him for years, as his thousands of art pieces are successfully hidden by his friends and colleagues from Nazi acquisition and looting. Picasso, Juan Gris, Sonia Delaney, Georges Braque and other noted painters continue to exhibit at "The Salon des Independents," in Paris.

In Paris, despite Hitler's warning that all "Decadent Art" will be burned or trashed by his troops. These exhibits represent the brave French and European painters of the decade, who despite Hitlerian warnings of censorship and destruction of their, Artworks. They defy his dictates to successfully express themselves under the protective umbrella of the French Government at "The Salon des Independents" at the Grand Palais in Paris.

However, many other artists lose all their works to this war, never to see the light again in art museums or public exhibitions. Their works are coveted for years by greedy persons, who thought they had the right to the spoils of war. Because of this the artworks become under-exhibited and therefore, undervalued in time. When they finally come to light many years later from independent owners they are re-appraised.

Some artists are given the Hitlerian stamp of approval such as artist Emil Nolde, considered a religious painter by Hitler, who illustrated scenes from the Bible. These primitive, heavily outlined, figurines in black somehow appealed to Hitler's sensibilities. Cartoon-like in many ways; these small paintings usually under 4x6 inches, gain a place in his hallway, at his residence in Dachau. As time passes and the, "Degenerate Art Exhibitions" of 1938, in Berlin gave way to other events, the German people forgot about these painters. Hitler and his Gestapo have staged exhibits in order to taunt, mock and destroy any works of art deemed degenerate to his "Aryan Nation" ideology. These include works by Yves Tanguy, Jacob Lipchitz, Salvador Dali, Sonia Delaunay, Juan Gris, Henri Matisse, Marc Chagall et al. Later revived by European galleries as greats after the end of WWII; these artists suffered enormous deprivation and censorship during this war climate. It covers their works with dark, obscure feelings from repressed, disciplined Aryans, too uptight to honor or celebrate their works. Any Jewish artist exhibited by Hitler, was then considered cannon fodder for his regime. If they did not emigrate quickly many of them would have perished in the concentration camps.

The Gestapo often hunted them down and killed them, particularly after an offhand remark by Adolph Hitler at one of these receptions. These were held in the Armory in Berlin monthly. This creates an atmosphere in the art world of suspicion, fear, and terror which lasts throughout the Reichdom.

Eventually Yves Tanguy, Marc Chagall, Franz Kline and many others escape with forged papers to New York. As they enter Manhattan society with its wealthy socialites, art collectors, such as the renowned Peggy Guggenheim, these people house, feed and clothe the émigrés. As refugees from a tidal wave of Nazi genocide, they can now earn a living in the United States. Utilizing FDR's program called the WPA, at Art Students League in Manhattan, these refugees have an opportunity to teach their trade on West 57th street near 5th Avenue.

SIENA

Corporal Al Downey has gone on a fact finding mission for the 3rd regiment. As he wanders down the narrow, cobblestone pathways of this ancient city of Siena, he finds a small Trattoria for a coffee. While there, resting after his arduous walk, he is tipped off by a local paisano, that a wealthy socialite is visiting from Manhattan. He trudges up the hundreds of steps Southward, leading to the entrance of this magnificent old cathedral, sunlight and golden in the distance. He eventually finds her standing near the altar in Saint Catherine's of Siena Cathedral, wearing a white mantilla with understated, Oleg Cassini beige, silk suit. Not shy, he introduces himself to her in the apse of the cathedral, shyly at first, twirling his dress blue officers hat around over and over in his hands searching for the right thing to say to this beauty. Finally, he gently doffs his hat, exchanging pleasantries for awhile. He invites her to coffee at a local ristorante in late afternoon.

After some time, he decides to exchange confidences about Ike's plan to evacuate orphans. She seems interested in participating despite terrible risks. He explains in greater detail how the Third Regiment will airlift the innocents from Nazi territory.

They will utilize; planes, trains and automobiles to move them out as rapidly as humanly possible. She is amazed at the urgency of this situation. It makes her gasp for breath to think of this atrocity happening within German borders.

Saving the lost and abandoned children of this war quickly, prior to Hitler's seven percent solution becomes imperative. They agree to meet in Siena several times more over Cappuccino, at the local "Trattoria

Annunziata", in the winding, narrow, cobblestone streets of Siena. She is always elegant, classy and respectful towards the soldiers. Together they formulate more cogent and cohesive plans. It is a great risk for Mrs. Ricci to participate in this venture. Al informs her that the Gestapo will follow her to the," Ends of the earth," for aiding these innocents. She gladly accepts this challenge. This woman is a gutsy dame. She joins forces with a friend, the famous clothing designer. A Spanish immigrant herself, Mrs. Carolina Herrera clothed and fed about two hundred little souls for a time. She also provides another villa in New York for them to retreat to for several months in the winter of 1936.

Hitler did not see children as innocents but blamed them constantly for his own foibles. His vengeance was so brutal that even his close associates began to see the chinks his armor.

Ms. Ricci generously offers her penthouse in Manhattan for the cause. Hundreds of escapees of Hitler's quest for annihilation by the Gestapo, are funneled through her ivory tower in Manhattan proper from 1938-1942.These émigrés of the war had a good and honorable friend in Mrs. Ricci. After due process at Ellis Island, these children were farmed out locally to many Manhattan socialites. They protected them en masse from harm. Celebrities, designers, and other like-minded Humanitarians worked together to be sure these refugees were properly placed in loving homes. Meanwhile they were schooled by private tutors by; Ms. Gloria Vanderbilt, Ms. Christina Ricci, Ms. Diane Von Furstenberg, Mrs. Caroline Herrera al. Later after acclamation to a strange culture, these "Orphans of the storm" were placed with waiting families in Manhattan and surrounding boroughs. No émigré child was left without a permanent home in America. This system worked like a charm.

Other artists and sculptors found solace and comfort under FDR's sponsorship from the WPA. He develops a Bill in Congress which allows artists in New York to work for the WPA, thereby working for a real living wage, surviving in one of the toughest towns in the US. Many artists, like Marc Chagall et. al worked for the WPA as Art Instructors in Manhattan to earn a decent wage.

TAIL-SPIN

It is October 14th,1933, Adolf Hitler has announced that he is withdrawing from the League of Nations. He adds that if the League attempts to improve sanctions with his new Minister General Werner von Bloomberg, that he would order German troops to fight. A new election is held in Germany. They expected 99% of the populace to go to the polls. Some ninety-five percentile of all German voters approved Hitler's decision to walk out of the League of Nations.

In 1934, Hitler announces that he is combining his office of Chancellor with the Presidency. He then appoints himself der Furher by crowing his head with a laurel wreath.

The Straussenkampfer have beaten the demonstrators about this illegal act. The Gutten had come to power.'Wir wollen das Gesetz-sans Mord und Totschlag." (We want power—otherwise death and destruction) was chanted by storm troopers.

Thirty-eight million Germans had said yah! Now the self-crowned Furher required every German officers to swear allegiance to him.

Now all over Germany, in theaters, restaurants, cafes bore signs— Juden Unerwunscht (Jews not Welcome). Nazi Messerschmitt fighter planes in the Luftwaffe were prepared to battle Britain's antiquated Tiger Moth bi-planes.

Winston Churchill pushed for Britain's rearmament. Neville Chamberlain remained convinced that Hitler would never attack France, England or the Low Countries. He saw Hitler hell bent on Russia not the West.

But on July 25th, Hitler sent some assassins to the Austrian government offices to kill President Dollfuss, the Chancellor of Austria. They did not accomplish their task. These assassins were caught and summarily executed.

Two years later Germany has tail-spinned into a Great Depression in 1935.Then Winston Churchill banned the sale of all aircraft to foreign nations. It was a total ban to any aircraft deliveries abroad. British intelligence ferreted out the information that over eight thousand German pilots were now trained.

At the League of Nations, Churchill stated, "If you want to stop war, you gather such an aggregation of force that the aggressor, whoever he may be, will not dare challenge. It is no use disguising the fact that there must be and ought to be deep anxiety in this country of Germany, which we will live to see, but we must consider that at present two or three men, in what may well be a desperate situation, have their grip on the whole of that mighty country."

March 16th,1935 Hitler ordered conscription of all youth. Hitler declared to England that the Reich had achieved parity with Great Britain, as far as their respective air forces were concerned in a meeting with Simon and Eden at the Chancellery. Lloyd George declares that Germany has been treated as a pariah. Baldwin argues in the House of Lords against the increased production of aircraft to combat Hitler.

Mussolini at this time is committed neither to Germany or the democracies. 'The Duce", admires Hitler's style but worries about Austria's fate. He knows the Furher had designs on it.

May 21st, Hitler assures France that Germany never dreamed of threatening other countries. He removes all claims on "Alsace Lorraine." Alsace became an escape route through the hills of Spain to freedom.

He is right. In Vienna, the Nazis storm the streets clubbing Austrian pedestrians, who fail to greet them with the stiff armed Hiltergrass.

General Bloomberg, the War Minister is now designated Commander in Chief of the Navy and Werner von Fritsch, the army. Goering heads the Luftwaffe; Raeder the Navy. Joachim von Ribbentrop is the Reich's Ambassador at large?

Churchill is being referred to in the House as a 'Scaremonger,' by

Baldwin and many others. On June 18th, 1935 an Angle-German Naval Agreement is signed. Hitler has spent eight-hundred million this year. That's 3.9 billion on arms alone. The League of Nations votes to impose economic sanctions on the Italians.

The Rome-Berlin Axis is formed. Mussolini has planned an invasion of Ethiopia. When Haile Selassie's capitol fell in Ethiopia to the Third Reich, The League of Nations had been destroyed as a "force of peace."

Nazi aggression is now seen on the Rhineland, which had been formerly guarded night and day, by the Austrian Security forces, continually to ensure security for the seaports. Churchill went home to "Chequeen's", the country house of the Prime Minister to prepare an address. Churchill sees Hitler's speeches as," Comfort for everyone on both sides of the Atlantic who wishes to be humbugged."

The Fuhrer loathes Churchill and always speaks of him with undisguised malice. "The gift Churchill possesses is to lie with a pious expression on his face and to distort the truth. His abnormal state of mind can only be explained as symptomatic of either a paralytic diseases or a drunkard's ravings. Only the Churchill clique will stand in the way of peace."

Churchill sounds his trumpet for three years but is silent about vying for office. "Asking Hitler to withdraw from the Rhineland is like asking Rasputin to use a knife and fork."

WHITEWASHED

There is a farmhouse in Alsace Lorraine. This beautiful, mountainous region at the base of the Alps, a French Protectorate is now called Lichtenstein. On it live twenty people; sisters, brothers, wives and husbands, some children, all Schmidt's.

Their farmhouse has a plain, whitewashed, oak paneled exterior. Inside there are various framed embroideries with old German sayings, surrounded by entwining perennials.

The screen door flings open as Harry Schmidt returns from a long day in the fields, wiping the sweat off his neck, with his white handkerchief. He is in his overalls with a white t-shirt. It is around ten in the evening. He places his straw, boater hat on the rack at the front screen-door.

Frustrated, hungry, he seats himself at the head of the table. Then with his clenched fist pounds on the oak planks saying, "Where's my dinner? Schnell! Schell!" The table reverberates with impatience.

Mary runs in from the backyard screen door to the dining room. She suppresses a worried expression knitting her brows. "Harry, I'm so sorry. I got carried away with the gardening. What do you desire?' "I don't know, you're the cook," scratching his belly. "Where is my dinner? Schnell! Schnell!" pounding his fist on the table. Harry gets up from the chair, taking out a corncob pipe. While lighting it, he moves into the living room for now, ignoring her. He sits in his favorite easy chair. To pacify him, she prepares a plate of braunschweiger, mustard and sweet pickles. They are placed quickly in front of him. A small loaf of pumpernickel bread is sliced. He begins to munch. "Where's my drink?" A bottle of Jägermeister is produced with a shot glass from the cupboard, by his wife Mary. He immediately downs the shot," Ah!" sitting back.

Mary's particular beauty lies in her long hair, which she has grown past her waist. She coils it, plaited on the top of her head, affixing stray stands with hair-combs. She wears a small flowered, cotton print dress.

Maria, his granddaughter is twirling around and around in a chair making herself dizzy. "Hi gramps!" Harry perturbed, "Stop that child! You are making me dizzy. "Maria puts her feet on the ground grinding to a halt. "Okay" Mary peers into the living room," I am on the phone. Do you want some Limburger?" "That's better than nothing. Maria do you want some cheese?" "No thanks, that stuff is stinky. I'll have a coke." At nine she has definite tastes. On the radio is heard," Ach der Lieber Augustine, Augustine ..."

Harry waits few minutes, then enters the kitchen where Mary is busily cooking on the stove.He searches for food, sour-faced, in the fridge. "Mary, why didn't you get the right pickles?" wincing, "I asked for sweet gherkins. What are these Mary?" pointing to a large jar grumbling.

"Harry, some of our guests like dill pickles. You can't always have it your way. Here I will fix another plate for you.' she leaves the boiled meal in the huge metal pot. Her specialty is corned beef and cabbage. Mary hails originally from Longford, near Three Mile House in Ireland. That farm was abandoned years ago when the Famine swept over the plains in the 1890's.

"I hope that curbs your appetite until dinner," Mary. Harry," Ah this is good." Maria runs in, stealing a slice off Harry's plate, running back into the living room.

"Wonderbra, wunderbar, what a perfect night for love," is heard on the radio in the distance. Maria inquisitive," Where did you find that corny station grandma?" "Your grandfather wants to hear his music. It's the only station with German songs he loves. "Never mind the dinner Mary. I will eat this. There is a guest coming tonight." He checks his silver watch and chain. "He has papers for me to sign."

Outside a tall man arrives at the front door in a dark storm. Under his raincoat, he carries a long, rolled up, manuscript tied with a golden chord and tassel. He uses the door knocker to rap. Maria playfully runs to the door, opening it so quickly no one can stop her. Mary walks into the living room, wiping her hands on her apron. Ria is attracted to the golden tassel, "What's that?" "This young lady, is a very important document. It took me a long time to find it. It is very old, almost a hundred years or more. Where is your grandfather?'

Maria points to the still preoccupied Harry, munching his appetizer. Mr. Cohen enters the room to greet him," Ah, Harry my old friend." "Can't you see I am eating my dinner? grumpy. Mary bring us another chair." "Will you try some sausages?" Mr. Cohen laughing, "I have eaten." He unties the parchment, unrolling it carefully. It is an enormous onionskin paper. Maria fascinated, sits next to Harry. Mary enters the room with a cut glass, decanter of Sherry, with two small, crystalline glasses, on a silver, heirloom tray.

Harry stares blankly at the parchment. "What is this? I don't have my glasses." Maria stares at his bald head," Yes you do, Grandpa they're right on top of your head." Harry wakes up," Oh yes, yes, there they are child." He stares blankly at the parchment," I can't make head nor tails of it. Can you read it to me?" with innocent blue eyes. Mr. Cohen gets on one knee reading it aloud to him. Harry scratches his head. Maria plays with the tassel. She then places her hands under her chin intently listening, to try and gather the gist of it.

At nine–years-old this is difficult. Mary pours the sherry into the glasses. "This is a special occasion. "Harry throws up his hands in frustration," Ach der Lieber!" He takes his white handkerchief out of his overall pocket, wiping his face. He blows his nose, dabbing his eyes in frustration. "Pardon me, I have a cold," to his Attorney. "It's all Greek to me. I am too old to understand it I suppose."

Sitting back in his chair at the table. "No you aren't grandpa", Maria playfully. Mary then pours two shot glasses of Jägermeister.

"Try this", to Mr. Cohen. "Thank you, I think I will try that. What is it?" "It's traditional bitters. Down the hatch!" to Mr. Cohen. Harry stares point blank at the document," I am confused." "Not to worry old friend. It's good news. Ria conceals grins, sensing the gravity of this situation. "I will explain it to Grandpa. I got an "A" in Spelling," Maria grins.

Harry, sheepishly to Mr. Cohen, "You see, I can't read." "Well, it's the deed to your property. It's all right. You can keep it. And no one can push you off of it. All I need is your signature here."

Suddenly Mr. Cohen produces a black ink well, and large feather quill. Harry dips the feather in the well. Determinedly he makes a huge "X" on the document. Placing the feather down. "That is how I sign my name." Maria stares at him. "That's all right grandpa, "blowing her nose. "I have a cold gramps". "Why does everyone have a cold around here?" Harry is miffed, pounding his fist on the table.

Mr. Cohen, "Well, I guess I can make this work at the courthouse. Are you certain that you understand it's meaning? You can keep the house after all. That neighbor cannot push you off it, "Attorney Glenheim asks politely. "Harry starts up from his dining room chair," Yah, he thinks that because we are Christians here; that we cannot stay here. That man is an Atheist. He doesn't believe in God. He makes Mary and me miserable. Who does he think he is? Why, for example, can't we even walk past his house; he calls the authorities, saying I am pulling up his flowers or something awfully important! "Harry sits back now considering this unfortunate situation." "I am glad you came to our humble house. Now we can celebrate." Harry pours another round of Jägermeister.

Mr. Glenheim, "Thanks, but one is strong enough for me." He gets up to leave in the pouring rain. "Remember he can't make those charges stick," putting on his fedora. "I will defend you and your wife with this paper. It is almost as old as you are." Harry slaps his thigh, "That's a good one."

As the Attorney leaves, Harry finally stands up to shake his hand. He is pleased as Punch to get this news.

Maria runs over to stare out the window at the neighbor across the street. He is a bald, German man with a mean face in a black t-shirt. She continues staring at him intensely. "Maria get away from that window and come to dinner!," Mary Hunt calls to her sternly.

SOLDIERS *without guns*

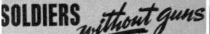

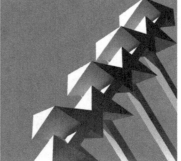

ALSACE LORRAINE

In the mountains of Alsace, Harry's mother Eleanor makes her candles of melted wax, hanging them on a thin cord to dry. They reside in the cobbled stone, brick home, near the edge of the River Rheims. The melting pot of black iron doubles as a soup container. It is sometimes so thin with only a few mustered up potatoes to share amongst twelve farmworkers. These are my grandfather's family, the Schmidt's. He was one of thirteen children. Harry wear blue jeans with suspenders and a white undershirt. He has an orange corduroy coat, his only winter coat. He wears heavy, work boots with thick, grey, woolen socks which help in the snowstorms.

Harry's bed, made of only straw, with a coarse, muslin cloth smells of bleach. In the Wintertime, for lack of flour and sugar at the farm, Harry Schmidt treks five miles, to the local village. He wears fingerless, denim work gloves, which turn his hands red and freezing.

The snow smarts his face, burning his lips raw; yet he still manages to bring home something. It is a small sack of gold coins.His mother cries for flour which hurts his heart. He makes this trek daily to feed thirteen souls.

These days in Alsace are the worst days this family has known. Their faces look hollow with pain, longing for fresh bread.

The outlaws who steal from the rich have become heroes to them. These men are sons of the farmers, who often raid the trains passing through the village which lie below the mountains of Alsace.

The farmers lined up in the freezing snow, some with only rags around their feet for shoes. Sacks of grain and flour are thrown at them gruffly. The oats and barley sustains them from starvation which sweeps over their lands in Lichtenstein. The German Depression is in full swing. These sons of farmers, dressed in overalls and plaid shirts, are now their folk heroes, although fierce bandits.

In the summer, the Brown shirts have begun to raid the bushels of hay, left tied in the fields. The boys throw the bales into their convoy trucks, laughing at the old man, who shakes his pitchfork at them. "Shisser," he screams as they steal all his profits. They pull away carelessly, arrogantly glaring back at him as if he was there only to aid them. In Winter the crops are frozen through. There were no bitter seeds left to plant.

It seems impossible to continue, but he must go on. In the early morning, at daybreak when the cock crows, many of the local farm owner's line the tracks along the center at the main station. Praying for bread, these farmers stand for hours, then like clockwork, the bandits raid the train cars. Men with hands covered in wrapped cloth reach out for sacks of grain heaved off the train. These pistoleros throw sacks of flour at them.

They have raided them from the conductor at gunpoint.

It's the German misery to be without grain or bread ten years. Without grub, many will die in the winter of 1936, on their farms so isolated from town. Harry and Ode Schmidt make a point of visiting town with their mule and cart, full of metal milk jugs. The unfed cows are still giving milk, just enough to keep them in kroner, but barely.

The Smiths travel weekly to town with their oxcart. It ambles down dirt roads many miles into the village. Then Ode leaves Harry there as he scrambles up some kroner, by selling his own teeth which he has pulled out.

The girls Barbara and Eleanor find spools of brightly, colored thread so the girls can mend more clothing. They take in for a few schillings. Barbara takes mending from the townsfolk, home with her to the farm. She is known also for her embroidery and lacework, which is so fine. She sells it for many kroner. Sometimes the entire clan depend on her beautiful, fine work for flour and sugar.

Satisfied with a few items, the brothers and sisters travel back towards Alsace. At exactly four o' clock, Barbara clangs the triangle outside on the ranch porch proudly. The workers gleaning in the fields stop, mop their necks, often burnt red from the sun. They walk into a huge, porch area where a large bent-wood table seats twelve. On the table are fresh, buttermilk biscuits, eggs, and even ham on special occasions.

This tribe is Christian, so they bow their heads and say grace daily. In the city, grace is frowned upon by sophisticated folks. City folks have eschewed religious practices, many of which are now banned by the Gestapo.

Mary makes the Sign of the Cross. Large, ceramic bowls are passed around Country Style. This family will survive, but Harry and Ode know they must leave their beloved Alsace soon, because the Brown shirts are gaining control of the city. Many Catholics have already left the city for America or other Catholic countries. They must decide soon to take all thirteen brothers and sisters to America before the deluge of Nazism drowns their countrymen.

It's a family necessity to sell this farm at the best price. Harry goes outside to smoke a corn cob pipe after supper, gazing at the verdant green hills, the white capped mountains he loves. "This family has owned this farm for centuries. Where will we go? "he ponders, kicking the gray, worn-out planks on the porch veranda. Ode and Barbara sit on the swing. She is reluctant to leave. Harry who served in the German Navy in WWI says," I have already done my duty. I will not follow this movement," stomping his heavy workbooks on the porch deck avidly. "This movement is gaining too much power. The city folks think they can have something for nothing. They are being fed pulp. Why do these Brown shirts sack up?" "Barbara, "Surely, they are not doing well themselves. These young boys are desperate."

They have been led to believe that the country now belongs only to the young. "What about us? We have worked this land for decades. Without us they would starve." Harry agrees, "We are the salt of the earth!"

"There is talk that they are actually rounding up people in the town,"

Ode grimaces. "Why?", puzzles Harry. 'Who knows why they take them to work camps daily," Ode. "Where will we go?"

Harry is knocking on doors, asking for more credit. He pulls at his pockets. He is lacking the kroner for a sack of flour. He often walks three miles to begin his day.

This family has only known farm life. None of these children has ever been to school. It is not mandatory in Germany or Alsace. The irony here is that Harry could never write at all. It simply was not required. He could only sign the deed to the land with an "X. "But his little granddaughter Maria will attain two Master's degrees, to tell his story in America.

TRI-CORNERED HAT

On Sunday morning, the entire family attends Saint Emydius Catholic Church. Evelyn is dressed in an elegant, navy blue suit, a netted hat with white gloves on, as is the fashion in the 50's. She sits next to her father Harry in the pew. Maria is all dressed up in deep, blue velvet, with a lace collar at age nine.

She kneels next to Evelyn. Harry is in a tweed suit with straw hat, sporting a blue and white bandana. He sits on the end of the pew kneeling, holding a prayer book in his hands. The Monsignor is dressed up in a long, black robe with a flowing fuchsia sash with tri-cornered hat. He passes by the front pew quickly. He glances at Harry, who is now a humble eighty-two.

"Do you know what you are doing wrong? You are holding the prayer book upside down!" the Monsignor chides him sternly. Harry look up with his trifocals amazed at this chastisement by the Monsignor. "I can't read," Harry replies simply.

He fumbles his glasses to disguise enormous embarrassment. "There is something wrong with his glasses," Evelyn, tears forming in her eyes, "Please father, he is eighty-two years old". Harry sits back in the pew quietly. He heaves a sigh, then takes out his white handkerchief wiping his brow, his hand shaking. Harry had never been to school in Germany. It was not mandatory for farm laborers.

EVELYN

I t is now 1938. There is a call to arms by FDR and Winston Churchill. Evelyn Schmidt, a German-American, is just a small town girl. She is tired of life on the farm. Evelyn sees nothing but adventure in these recruiters hanging posters in her village. She decides to volunteer for the WAVES, who are training in the San Diego harbor area. She packs her bags in Mankato, Minnesota, a small German farming community, in the Southern Quarter, of Blue Earth County.

For once in her short life, she is leaving this tightly knit community to do her service abroad. She will experience so much in so little time. She is told that she must face down six weeks of basic training, before she is assigned a station.

While in training, she specifically requests service near London. Due to her prior brilliant training; she is stationed in Liverpool by order of her Commander Schultz. Upon her arrival in London's Heathrow airport, dressed in her dark blues; she is met by an attaché, who takes her along with twenty other gals to their assignment post. As they travel by double decker bus through London Town; she notices the gas masks of the Londoners while passing them by on the cobblestone streets.

After a brief tour of London they arrive at the Excelsior Hotel in the center of London. They are served at tea time at 3 with fragile china cups, butter curls with lemon scones.

After awhile they adjourn to the anteroom for a conference. They are then briefed about the military might posted there. The US Army and Navy were sent there to bolster up the Naval forces.

The British Naval might have never replenished after WWI. A

Colonel with the US Navy shows a huge chart to them. The maneuvers of the ships are delineated carefully on charts with graphics, at the center of the room. She has been assigned to the USS Mississippi. This ship is a Destroyer, capable of three times the might of British ships stationed there.

Winston Churchill has to plead with Parliament to finance more Battleships, due to this mighty vison of the Incursion and Holocaust which he foresees. He pleads for years with Prime Minister Neville Chamberlain, who seeks appeasement of Adolf Hitler. It frustrates Churchill to such an extent, that the weight and gravitas of his voice rebound through the ancient chambers of Parliament. Eventually he convinces Parliament in Britain to see to it that ships are supplied for the Navy in the nick of time. But in truth, without the American backup plan of Tankards and Destroyers, there would have been no victory at sea.

At long last the ships are deployed to maintain security for all concerned. Hitler has sent his MIG fighter jets with bombs repeatedly to show the force of his Luftwaffe. The British respond in kind.

Evelyn a new WAVE, anxious to see her station, disembarks on the USS Mississippi. She then prepares for a long stay, unpacking the steamer trunk. She even brought her dishes.

A girl like Evelyn from a small village is dwarfed while

stunned by London. Excited by all the new sights and smells along the wharf; she slowly but surely develops a love of the British people. She is especially fond of the Cockney's, who Possess delightful charm and humor. She enjoys their down to earth ways. It makes her smile during grim days. She will pass by the open fish markets daily to find fresh mackerel, salmon and tuna for lunch.

As part of her duties, she also keeps the books for the ship which entails accounting skills which are her forte.

One night the ship is covered in ocean waves breaking over the deck, loudly crashing. The sound is so furious, Evelyn stares out her porthole window. Eventually the sea subsides after tons of breakwater fills the deck. She goes back to her books with a jaundiced eye slogging through the halls in heavy boots.

It takes these mighty battleship months to attain the reputation of honorable sea vessel, after numerous air attacks by the Luftwaffe. Seven MIG fighter jets swarm through the dark skies near Liverpool at 12 o'clock high. The machine gunners man the decks quickly. The gunfire pierces the silent seas for twenty minutes as MIG's explode in the air, with orange lights crackling around them. The debris falls in clumps around the ship, sinking further into the flashing, capped waves. Evelyn is struck by the drama and majesty of it all. Her cabin mates tease her no end. The other girls see her as a small town hick who guffaws at this adventure.

They all did, except for Ernie March. One Sunday on leave, she travels by bus to Hyde Park, with a girlfriend in uniform tagging along.

They decide to pack a picnic, while relaxing on the lawn. The weather is actually quite decent for October. Ernie spots her, with her black, raven locks, creamy tan skin. Her violet- blue eyes shine brightly, as she smiles a graceful smile at him. "Where are you girls stationed?" doffing his cap. He wears a tan uniform, which is befitting his station as an Ensign in the RAF. "I don't get to meet Americans very often."

Evelyn stands to shake his hand. He convinces them to come to tea at the local bistro. As they enjoy scones with a big helping of apricot jam, the conversation becomes full of tenacity. Ernie is chaffing at the bit to fly a mission into hell, to defeat the "Red Baron". The Red Baron has flown so many successful missions as a fighter ACE, that he is a man to contend with. All the men are talking about the Baron's exploits.

Ernie believes that he is the man to bring him down to size for the British RAF. Ernie considers himself to be somewhat of an aeronautics expert. "I can do whirligigs. Perhaps you girls would like to go for a spin sometime?" "Sure, when we can break away; we'll meet up with you in town", Evelyn smiles wanly. Her eyes dreamily glancing to the side. They part amicably, formally. The other girl is giggling. She sees their budding romance immediately.

After two weeks, a dance is organized onboard the ship without fail. The men prep a stage front and center. The microphones are set up mid-afternoon. All the girls are swishing their crinoline skirts around the cabin. They are donning real, silk stockings with seams down the back. Evelyn wears studded, pearl earrings. Her gown is soft, yellow crinoline, with three petticoats on a cinched waistband. Her hair smell of Maya perfume. Evelyn is half-Italian/half German with olive skin, blue-violet eyes, raven black hair. She is gifted with poise and a refreshing attitude. Eight o'clock rolls around slowly. The girls prep orderves down below. Several other ships have docked alongside. Guests are now pouring onto the main deck.

Pennsylvania 4-500, a Jimmy Dorsey Big Band tune, plays over the speakers on deck. The boys already dancing, swing with any dame they choose. Ernie spies Evelyn at the punch bowl drinking Suicide Punch. It is a concoction of the Southern unit. Ernie laughs openly at Evelyn's proud exclamation that she made up the punch bowl with plenty of Rum.

They dance all night. He is so enamored with this Italian- German beauty, he holds her too tight at first. It makes her nervous. She is still very innocent in the ways of the world. Ernie asks her out on the town. When he takes a leave next month, she accepts, smiling gracefully. Ernie courts her whenever he can. After six months, they are engaged.

Evelyn wears a white suit with a gardenia corsage, while Ernie is in his dress blues. Evelyn proudly holds her gardenia corsage for pictures. They find a Catholic Church in London for the ceremony. Soon they are together in Bristol by the Sea.

However, the Air Force has other plans for Ernie March. They make short shrift of their honeymoon. Ernie gets reassigned. He packs for London's Air Force Base. While Ernie stays in London; she discovers she is pregnant while onboard the ship. She carries on bravely, writing him letters from her cabin nightly. It is now December. The ship is frosted, colder than a well digger. Everyone is blowing hot and cold. News blares over the radio in the Control Room that Hitler is attacking London by airstrike again. The British are hunkering down for a real battle. The bombing of London has begun in full sway. Citizens run to underground tunnels; as sirens blare for hours in the darkened skies. The orders are "Lights Out".

Anxious for Ernie to meet her Italian relations; Evelyn plans a trip to meet her mother's family. Rosa lives in Cortona, Italy in the mountains near Venice. She receives a note from Ernie that he cannot go with her. His duty comes first in London. The air strikes are so fast and furious he must remain. Sadly, she goes by herself accompanied by an Italian friend Annette Gorgone. Traveling by "The Tube", then bus; they arrive after an exhausting excursion in Venice for a few days. All seems perfect until Evelyn spills her guts. She disagrees with a commandant in Piazza San Marco about his manners towards the Italians passing by. He keeps calling them pigs, slobs etc. loudly. Evelyn is unaware that the Reich has taken Venice by storm. She is arrested for talking back to him. Annette runs for help. But she finds none. It takes over two weeks of talking to the American Embassy to get Evelyn reprieved. Sad and disheveled, Evelyn is granted her freedom on strict instructions that le Donne return to their ship immediately.

Evelyn is so livid after this arrest; she begins to plot with Al Downey to take children out of Italy. They are being shot in the streets by Luftaffe, while eating garbage in place of food.

If they are orphaned by the Nazi incursion, their chances of any survivial are extremely limited.

Evelyn receives a letter overnight in a mailbag whilst onboard ship. She is asked to return to Roma. She will meet some underground workers. She agrees to travel by night. There are so many dangers; Al has taken many precautions to secure the mission. While in Rome they agree to meet at the Vatican by phone. Vatican City is still neutral territory; therefore anyone can travel there unencumbered. As Evelyn travels by bus through the streets there, she sees the old marble statues in rubble, defeated by the Luftwaffe. The ancient pillars are felled by bombing, debris all around. Children scamper through this dangerous rubble. These are the Orphans of the war, with no place to go. They have acquired tough exteriors, wizened, crinkled faces. Most are expert pick pockets. The American soldiers don't seem to mind giving them chocolate bars from the PX. These children are abandoned by the Italian government. They are lost among the conquered temples of ancient Rome. They spend their time stealing from open market vendors. These children run up to Al tagging along with his mates begging for lire. After awhile Al gets the notion to write a long letter to General Eisenhower about this situation.

He meets Evelyn in early morning, for a planning session with two other soldiers, near Centro, in a Trattoria. They formulate some plans to move hundreds of these orphans out quickly, vite vite! The "Seven Percent Solution" comes down like a tidal wave.

Hitler's madness has increased steadily. He screams, stomps his black boots; his mouth frothing, continually, for no apparent reason. He is like one possessed of a devil. This man casts no shadow. It became painfully obvious to his fellow Gestapo officers, that he has lost his mind entirely. Several Gestapo agents plan to get rid of him. But how? Surrounded by a loyal guard, which is almost impenetrable, they think this idea is futile. However, several of them branch off with a firm resolution to have him removed. This becomes "Valkyrie', a movement of insiders in the Reich to eliminate this embarrassing undisciplined, leader.

When Hitler issues a proclamation on onionskin paper that all children are to be killed, it is the last straw. He insists that all children under sixteen who are not white, Aryan children must be gassed to death in chambers, located in Buchenwald. The Gestapo are shocked but gravely silent, cowed by his screaming and terrorism. This is his "Seven Percent Solution." To eliminate all stray children, steal non-Aryan children from their homes. To gas them in chambers, in Buchenwald Concentration camp.

Al with the Third and Fourth regiment must move quickly. These soldiers are busily finding ways to forge documents in Roma.

They seek out a noted Archbishop, renowned for his Humanism. They ask him for precious documents to evacuate these marked children readily. Believing that an Archbishop is impervious to arrest, they approach him. As they enter the enormous marbled hallway of the Vatican, they walk though Renaissance halls of gilded edges with brown marbled porticoes. They have a look of urgency on their faces. The Swiss Guard of red and gold, escort them to a huge room lined in red-veined marble pillars. There in the center of the room is a marbled Renaissance desk with gilt edges. In a 16th century wooden, Spanish style chair with tassels and brocade pillows sits an Archbishop. In front of him are a quill pen and inkwell. He has been briefed about this evacuation through the Holy See. Busily he signs parchment proclamations for these men to carry with them.

Suddenly, in bursts a Gestapo agent, a Colonel Klingmann. He takes off his black, leather gloves, throwing them on the ground in Mediaeval style. This declares his intent to battle with them.

One of his fellows takes out a luger shooting at the hand of the Archbishop, wounding him. He shrieks. A huge, portal door opens with children pushing it open. They run to the Archbishop surrounding him. They believe he will be murdered. This stops the Commandant from further shooting. These children block the desk with their bodies. This Commandante backs off for the moment, surprised at their resolve to protect him.

"What is the meaning of your prescence here?" "You have no jurisdiction in Vatican City", another priest inquires sharply. "We have orders to stop this immediately from der Furher." This soldier then aims at a thirteen-year-old, shooting him in the arm.

The child, Paolo grasps his arm in pain yelling loudly. The soldier then aims at the priest near the Archbishop. "Put that gun away subito sir." The Swiss Guards enters surrounding them. They force them to drop their arms. The Commandant is startled. "But we have a proclamation here from der Furher to arrest this priest. Have you no understanding? He must be taken in. These are forgeries." Colonel Klingman grabs a few documents, throwing them at the Swiss Guard. The Swiss Guard hands the documents over to the Archbishop, who sits there with a bleeding hand. "Sir, your papers.", calming, complicity

Colonel Klingman is taken outside by two guards carrying spears. The enormous doors close slowly. Outside the children can hear a dull thud as the Archbishop hits the floor in pain. "Quickly, quickly before other men come," they usher them out the back door, running them down a long hallway. It seems an interminable hall while dozens of children search for hiding places in Vatican City.

These dozens of children, soon to be thousands or evacuees', are sequestered for a time in a convent. There, they are given alternative clothing. The convents along the sides of the Vatican plaza, take in many of these orphans. They spend hours forging the needed papers. The clothes are donated then dyed with boot polish. The children are given English lessons nightly after dinner, a simple soup and bread, with some occasional slabs of meat. For hours they are drilled with English vocabulary to prepare for their flight out of hell. The nuns know that those who do not escape, will be taken to Buchenwald and exterminated one and all. Already thousands have been gassed in the chamber in Auschwitz and Birkenau. This is coming down like helter skelter for these children of the war. Hitler has commanded that all non-Aryans be exterminated immediately. The nuns are hurriedly preparing these evacuees. In a few days they will be escorted proudly by the Third and Fourth regiments located in Roma outside the outskirts of Vatican City. Thousands will be shuttled in train cars with Allied soldiers, guarding the cattle cars, as they guide them across the borders into Free France then London. Some will be placed in England, others Manhattan. On the orders of General Eisenhower, a proud German-American, these children will eventually experience liberty.

Harry Schmidt, after he emigrated from Germany to Minnesota, had organized a Farmer's Union there, to ward off smugglers. It was during the Great Depression Era of the 1930's." I'll be damned if these smugglers, steal my goods, now that I'm in America," he would fume. "I have farmed here twenty years, the length and breadth of this land. I have traced it's borders with my shoes. I have gulped the soil. It is rich in minerals, fertile. I know how to farm. Just give me a piece of land. I'll make something of it," shaking his fist at the sun. "That is my birthright!" Harry yells in his fields.

He had fought these culprits bitterly for over twenty years. It was discovered that these crooks hailed from New York City.

Later when he passes away, hundreds come to his funeral at Saint

Emydius Catholic Church in Lynwood, California. When Mary Hunt Schmidt, his companion of over fifty years passes, she receives a queenly funeral as well, one year later. The doctor says that she simply died of a broken heart.

Mary Hunt Schmidt and her daughter by adoption Kathryn Marie Schmidt, smuggle immigrants out of Germany for years after WWII, by forging papersalong with other documentation. They work at the kitchen table for hours. I witnessed this myself for many years as a young child.

Eventually in her eighties, Kathryn is put under House Arrest for smuggling a Jew, in danger of annihilation by the Germans.

She is placed under House Arrest for five years, by Downey Police Department which sports a Nazi advocate named Otto, who virulently goes after her, in her eighties at her home in California. Katy believes in her heart that she is doing a noble thing. These men refuse to recognize her humanitarian efforts to save the life of an innocent women. Thelma is being persecuted simply because she happens to be Jewish. These are not the times of compassion and humanity in the United States. We have forgotten the hard and bitter lessons of WWII. Who would put a Nazi Commander in charge in the Police Department but an ignorant Mayor? When we forget the past, we are truly repeating it's mistakes. It's time to wakeup about immigration. Many of these people are under the gun in their home countries. These émigrés are desperate to get away from persecutors, who defy their religious beliefs.

Since Kathryn could no longer leave her home whilst under House Arrest, I bring food and medicine to her door for years. She passed away at eight-nine years of age in 2006.She is buried in the family crypt.

RIVERS OF FIRE

In late August, a brigade of Brown shirts raids the fields firing them with torches. The farmers are aghast at this senseless act.

They scramble to the river for buckets of water, making a line to douse the fires. One Brown shirt erects a wooden sign on the property, 'Property of the German Government." Harry is livid. "Since when does the government own our land? This is Alsace, this is shisser! You do not belong here. Get out." Again Harry has miscalculated as three more convoys arrive. The Brown shirts throw curses at them," You are a foolish old man, "one scoffs. "This is a new world. You must work for us now! "to Harry.

They do not know now, that their future leader is a sixteen-year old Brown shirt, living in a small town near Auschwitz.

The next summer, the crop is plentiful, full of golden, green corn and hay. But all the Schmidt's are gone.

They have fled the Vichy government through the mountains of Italy to Belgium, taking a steamer to the coastline, to America's Ellis Island.

Someone has told them of rich, fertile soil in Minnesota. So they pack up old trunks with china and silver, all they can take. The journey is over one hundred miles into Belgium. They arrive worn out but eager to leave their beloved country. Harry has managed to arrange passage for four Italians as well, marrying Rosa Zavalla to smuggle this wealthy Italian from Cortona, out of Italy, through the mountain pass. Things are much different there. Mussolini has taken over, only to later mimic Adolph Hitler, a twenty-one-year upstart, who is the leader of the brown shirts now, gaining power daily.

This Catholic family are fed up. They resort to selling everything they can; jewelry, crystal, china bowls, porcelain and watches for fare on the steamer. To leave they have to go separately from different locations for safety. The Gestapo is watching them at all times. Rosa has always lived in high society in Cortona in the mountains. She has met Harry Schmidt on a trip to Southern Spain. She is not enamored of him. He sees her earnest desperation to leave Western Europe, as signs of the takeover are imminent. The news was censored, but news from the country people spread like a wildfire. Strangers passing through the small villages tell their stories in Hofstra's over steins of Pauli Girl's beer. These arrogant lack shirts are closing in.

Ode will return with Myron, his brother, as fighter pilots for the American government to give Hitler back some hell!

BLOOD OATH

G reta Hrothgar discreetly takes a blood oath with the Nazi Party in Berlin. She has vowed it over a Bible turned upside down, near a Convention center in the Eastern Part of Berlin.

She is now part of eight, carefully chosen Gestapo Party members who regulate the arts in the city. She claims it will avenge their tribe; to take a blood oath, drinking a dram of their mixed blood. She throws back her tresses, downing a flute of real blood-work.

Greta has agreed in written script, in her own blood to torture, maim, and decapitate all offenders of the Aryan Nation. She is proudly wearing a ballroom style, beige, silk-lined, cape to the event with black stack heeled shoes. She purchased them from a fashionable German store, especially for the occasion. She swears on a stack of Bibles to avenge, avenge, avenge.

She has taken this oath to get back at her Jewish husband, whom she often claims cheated on her repeatedly. Greta Hrothgar is a determined woman of German heritage. She sees the world through a glass darkly. Only vengeance would rid her of her troubles. She even sets up five of her husband's cousins in Poland, during the course of this vengeance. She is deemed an untouchable by the Jews, who are savvy about her activities. Shunned in mixed company, she goes on. She often plays confidence woman to them in order to garner information.

She relays quickly by phone, messages to her cohorts in the city center. It makes her feel important to set up her husband's cousins from long distance. She loves to see him cry.

Greta has a peculiar facility to track down others. She is attracted to a handsome Graphic Designer, half her age. He is recently engaged to a beautiful, innocent blonde girl whom he adores. He is sitting on top of the word with his career, a bright future.

He had been commissioned by Mr. Albert Speer, architect for the Reich, to design various modern apartments for the Gestapo. Greta hears of these architectural designs. She tugs at her husband's sleeve. "Daddy I want to show my paintings in those apartments. Help me please. He has to show my works in those apartments or I will die. You must come with me to convince David that I am the artist he needs, to fulfill this dream. "Well I don't know, der Furher is not my cup of tea and neither is Mr. Speer, a spoiled, rotten punk if I ever saw one." "You're entitled to your opinion dear, but if I don't get this commission I will die." "Well, you can go over there if you want to, but I think it will be a waste of your time." He grabs his coat from a coat rack, putting on a rain slicker and fedora hat searching quickly for the studio door. Greta makes a few calls.

It's Sunday morning! She is so excited, she is up and about at 4am making Cappuccino. As she sips her coffee, she plans her wardrobe with great care. "I must not appear to be presumptuous" she schemes, nor too reluctant. She wraps her hair in braids around her head with multi-color ribbons weaving through them.

Then dons an all-black ensemble from head to toe. In her black leggings, skirt, blouse and petticoat, she has an aura of death. As she heads out, she blows a kiss to her husband sound asleep. She walks to her nearby neighbor pounding loudly on the solid, metal factory door. He opens it graciously, but surprised at her early morning visitation. "Greta it's only six o' clock. Man needs his rest," heaving a sigh. She stomps her pointed toed slipper, "Yes I know that but I simply must see you now." "As you like, but make it brief. I have a lot of work to do today for my finals. I am in competition with my blueprints for this commission." "Be Brief, but I have oodles to tell you! "Be brief!" I can't make this brief. Why do you shun me?" "You know, looking him up and down in his plain backed chair. "You've changed. You used to be so nice. Now you're so conceited and rotten, I just can't stand you at all." "I'm sorry to hear that," sipping his coffee calmly, rolling his eyes towards the heavens.

"Well okay I have a present for you," Greta produces a small, silver, gun from her black, clutch purse. "Is that a gun for me?" he glares at the small, silver pistol." I want that commission and you have to get it for me. Do you understand me?' stomping her black, pointed shoe. "Is it that important to you? I don't think you and I would get along at all". "Wouldn't we? Well maybe, if I show you a little leg we would, "grinning, raising her skirt with her opposing hand.

"No thanks, I'm engaged." "Oh that, well you'll get over that." She sits on a chair opposite him staring at his midsection. "You're not in shape are you. Flabby I see, but I can correct that. My men are in better shape. You should be ashamed of yourself." At this remark, David stands, up walking away, "Greta this is getting us nowhere. Now if you want to act like civilized people fine otherwise, I have work to do." He continues to drink his coffee wondering what he has to deal with here. "Very well, I'll make you a proposition. You pay me ten thousand dollars for two of my paintings and I'll let you rub my backside for two hours." "Ridiculous, I am not interested in your backside." "Oh no? You were the other night. "Sitting down staring at her. "What night was that?" heaving a sigh. "Why can't you play along? I'm not used to being turned down, you idiot! "Not now! As I say, I'm busy today," he turns away from her. "Look why are you so unreasonable? I can get my husband to convince you. He is very convincing. He has many important friends." "Does he? Well I don't know a one of them, now please leave me in peace. I am quite sure that you have better things to do."

"Drafts," stomping her foot. I didn't think it would be this way. Why are you so stubborn?" She turns toward the wall, looking at her feet. She glares at the ground for awhile. "Greta will you leave?" "No damn it! I won't. I came here to do a deal and I will do a deal if it hurts." "Greta please leave!" He saunters calmly to the door, opening it for her to exit. She just stands there frozen.

He grabs her by the forearm frustrated; trying to escort her out the door. It is now 8am." Look, look I'll make you another deal, but please, please don't tell my husband," coyly. "You can have sex with me whenever you want, if I can just have this commission. You'll get bored with that girl soon anyway. She kicks a dust bunny on the concrete floor. Surprised he just glares at her poker face," I'll think it over.

Now will you please leave?" David feels affronted but tries to suppress his true feelings "If you don't deal with me I'll just die. Everyone makes fun of me here. I really don't fit in. I feel like a terrible misfit with no honor. I need this commission." "Okay Greta, I promise to think about it," showing her the one more time." What does it take to make you leave?" She grabs him by the belt and pulls her towards him giving him a hot kiss on his lips. He is surprised. "Well I, well I … She begins to disrobe. "Greta not now!" "Why not now?" Embarrassed by her sudden aggression. "I choose who I make love to." He sits down affronted. She straddles him pulling this hair. "You're so cute and I'm so little. I could make you wince in pleasure."

"Okay, just one, unbuttoning his trousers. He gives her a quickie. She licks her chops, pulling her skirts down. "Where can I wash? I've never been in here before? "Over there" pointing to a huge metal sink. She practically jumps in, splashing cold water all over her genitals. My husband says if I do this I won't get pregnant." "Greta, you didn't wear protection? "Sometimes I forget!" "Now will you go?" standing up. "In a minute, I want to ask you something." "What is it?" sighing. "Do you love me yes or no?" folding her arms akimbo. "No, I don't. You came on to me. Get real!" "Real, what's real about you?'" You pretend to be a gentleman but I can see you're not!" She straightens out the seams of her black stockings carefully.

"Okay, I'll go, but I'll tell my husband how you treated me." She turns to leave." And one more thing, I didn't enjoy it." She turns near the entrance of the art studio. "On second thought, here's a surprise." She shoots her small, silver gun at his head, grazing his forehead. He grabs his head, the blood begins to ooze through his hand. He looks at his hands, they are now covered with his blood.

She slams the cold, metal door shut. She runs to get her husband. He comes along reluctantly putting his suit coat on hurriedly.

She opens the door with a key that she stole from his bureau. "There he is, now finish him off!" Greta demands, glaring at her dirty work.

The blood seeps from his face onto the floor quickly. The studio floor is covered in blue-red blood. 'Finish who off? I don't see anything here," he gives her a sheepish grin. "I am so tired of cleaning up after you Greta!" Sullenly, he turns David's body over. It smacks the floor dully.

Seth stomps on his face with his leather shoe to destroy the evidence of the shooting. Then Seth spits on his face. Then he turns the body over again, dragging David out the door, face down to dispose of it.

Greta stands there delightedly, giggling as Seth drags David away. She rubs her hands together watching the scene, like a small child. "We won, we won!", Greta shouts.

Days later, the Gestapo arrive to investigate. They find no body, no blood, only curious explanations. A neighbor offers an account. They choose to reject it, as Seth palms them off with five thousand kroners. They lick their lips and depart. A neighbor hears the commotion calling the Gestapo again. He request to speak to the High Commissioner. Captain Moot, may I assist you?' "There is a steady commotion of screaming and noise next to my studio here. Can you check into it? I cannot work with this screaming. Can you check into this problem? immediately?"

"We will send a squad car to the address as soon as possible. You understand that this is low priority on our list tonight but rest assured we will deal with these people." The neighbor, aggravated, hangs up. He turns to his friend seated on a sofa in his painting studio, "He says he will send a unit out, but we must endure the screaming and raving for awhile." Meanwhile Greta has gone from cool killer to raving maniac, turning over her furniture, pulling the stuffing out of pillows and her sofa, even slashing it up with a knife. Then she sits on the dilapidated sofa with her arms crossed tightly. She gazes into space. Greta has returned to her studio after her husband has dragged David away, to hide his inert body.

Seth searching for a hiding spot, leaves the body, wrapped in a sheet in the hall for the moment. It is still early morning. The other tenants have not awakened. He knocks several times. No Answer. He uses a metal pin to enter the next door neighbor's art studio. Peering inside, he surveys the huge space. No one there. Finding that the tenant is not at home, he smiles wanly. Checking the space, he spots a Painter's coverall folded neatly over a chair," One size fits all. He puts it on quickly, over his suit. Hurriedly searching for someplace to stash David's inert body. He sees a huge wall panel near the kitchen sink. "Perfect," he chuckles to himself. He removes the drywall panel carefully, pushing the body behind the sink area awkwardly. The head keeps falling forward onto his own head. He pushes the body into an upright position. Then he replaces the drywall with hammer and nails carefully. "I hope that works, sheesh!" The panel fits back onto the wall perfectly. The one problem is the leaking blood under the uneven bottom of the panel. He takes a plastic bucket from under the tenant's sink sponging it down. He them removes the sponge from the premises, rinsing out the bucket. He laughs to himself. "This tenant is notorious for her lovers. Maybe he can get away with this. Why shouldn't they blame Griselda? What a perfect foil!" He leaves, closing the door gently behind him. Wiping off the remainder with a cloth he grabbed from her studio he stashes it in his coat pocket. Then he throws the cloth into the huge, metal, trash container outside. He decides to grab a cup of coffee to forget about his wife for awhile. He thinks to himself, "My Greta will go out of her way to extract her pound of flesh as she deems it."

Now Greta feels she has an inside move at these enormous arts building. She asks the caretaker, Andrew Schmidt, for an application form. She raps on his solid, metal door with great passion for ten minutes. "Wake up you lazy dog," she yelps at him. He looks into the peephole of the door. "What can I do for you? Are you a resident?" "No but I've come here to fill out the application to work here." "Well, where is it? I have only a little time. My husband is waiting in the car for me."

Andrew groggily searches for an application. He slides it under the door to her. She grabs a pencil from her black, quilted, designer bag scampering into the laundry room, her favorite squeaky clean place, to fill out the form. Within minutes she raps on Andrew's door again. He spies her outside. "Okay, just slide it under the door. I'll have Management look it over as usual. Then we will give you a call," Andrew miffed at her impudence.

She receives no call back. There are hundreds of applications piled on the Manager's desktop unrelentingly, collecting dust.

After a few weeks, she wanders over there all by herself, dressed in black garb from head to toe, her usual.

She waits until someone leaves the front security door, then sneaks past the alarm system. "Where is Andrew? She inquires around the building. "I have urgent business with him." Someone points out that he is on the roof; fixing an antenna for a resident named Thomas Carrillo. "Well how do I get up there?" she seems desperate, her lower lip quivering. "Just take the stairs up," a friendly artist guides her.

She, with superhuman energy, traverses eight flights of concrete stairs in a rage. She has an application in hand. There he is, fixing the antenna above Thomas' studio. It is a flat rooftop, over three hundred square meters wide. She runs up to him to scrap over her application. They get into a heated argument. He walks toward the edge of the building to get to the staircase to descend.

Within minutes Andrew's body falls off the roof, landing in the back of the building. Days go by before he is found. It is assumed to be a construction accident of some kind. No one even questions it. Her husband called it

"THE "FLYING WALLENDAS."

Her husband is admittedly no idea of a picnic. He normally acts on mob contracts, preferring to shoot his victims point black in the head, with a derringer, after making them beg loudly for their lives. It really turns him on to make them beg. He thinks drug dealers are low on the totem pole anyway. He carries this derringer in a red-brown shoulder holster, for thirty years' now, never leaving it behind.

Seth Hrothgar is the snarliest hit man in town. Famous in the casinos, he smokes Havana's, tells frequently off color jokes to amuse. He continually brushes back several strands of his thinning hair in order to cover his balding head. He is paid five thousand kronen per hit. Then he delivers parts of the body to his bosses regularly in brown paper.

This hit man is so dangerous, Gestapo agents fear him, often fleeing the scene pretending they did not see it. Police Lt. Gregson is such a man. A tall, blonde, Aryan type "He only hits his own" Gregson lies to himself while fleeing quickly. In fact, Seth hits all opposed to the mob, especially his wife's enemies, the innocent the more she goes after them. Lilliana, his wife, of over thirty years hates all innocent and good women. She never saw herself as attractive so needs to disfigure all good women who oppose her mob.

Then she will fill the air with horrible lies about her victim claiming they are prostitutes or hoares. It prevents sympathy forming in the minds of others. She will invent such fantastic tales of slander, it infects those around her. For some reason she has gotten away with numerous, degrading knifings. She really gets off on castrating the innocent, Once as she walked through the anteroom of the residence hall, where she and her husband lived for over thirty years. She is observed carrying a plastic bag full of eyes.

When questioned she stated flatly "These are only cat's eyes, not human ones." I use them for my experiments. Then she cackles throwing back her black, wavy tresses. She thinks nothing of cutting up small animals. One Landlord evicts her yearly, but she always comes back. Finally, the landlord is killed by Seth in a fit of pique.

She is particularly welcomed after the forced kidnapping of the prior Landlord's wife.

"We own this neighborhood", she cries out loudly, dressed in black from head to toe. "My daddy is a big mother fucker and anyone who opposes up get this", holding up a dead cat by it's spindly legs. She is even taking to drinking blood from a chalice, she ties it at her waist for show. With the long, black skirt, black leggings and pitch black shoes; she is quite the dismal sight, wandering aimlessly in the quad.

Griselda arrives back at her studio after a one night's stand somewhere in Soho. She has a long, red ponytail braided, a purple, lurex pantsuit with rhinestones everywhere. She fumbles in her black patent, leather bag for her keys, still drunk from the prior night's festivities. As she enters, she throws her bag onto the wine-red, velvet sofa. She goes into the powder room. Not noticing anything peculiar, she flops onto her sofa for a few winks after long, intense partying the night before. She decides in her half dreaming state to run off for a weekend with her new amour.

In a few days, the other neighbor notices a strange smell emanating from their shared wall. He telephones the owner, Swen. Swen gently knocks on Griselda's door in the early morning. No one is there.

In a wink, a plumber arrives. He observes the studio for awhile. It is deduced that the offensive odor is coming from behind the sink area. Swen gives the Plumber permission to open up the wall. Swen goes to get some work tools himself to aid him. Days later David's body is discovered in a state of rigormortis.

Griselda is questioned thoroughly, as she packs her bags to leave for her twenty-fifth honeymoon weekend. She is now listed on a "Person of interest list" for the time being. The police allow her the next fervent honeymoon trip.

Trevor, Greta's other next door neighbor is carefully hanging a show of his black and white, Expressionist Paintings. As he hammers, measuring the wall, she boldly walks into his open space. "You hoo! Look who's here!" she announces herself with flair." I hear that you are having an exhibit. But you didn't invite us. Now shame on you, I have to approve your work. No one has an exhibit here without my approval you know, waggling her finger in his face. Trevor is unaware that she is Nazi Party Monitor, of all things cultural, in this arts building.

Trevor laughs gamely. "Approval heh? Well then, what do you make of this one?" He takes a painting encased in birch wood flipping it towards her pivoting it on the floor. "Not bad, a tad specious!" staring bold faced at his works. "Greta you don't know what specious means." "Oh Trevor, you always make fun of me, just because I dropped out of school," sullen. She flings her black skirts to the side, like an enraged Flamenco dancer, strutting out with attitude.

"Greta don't take it so hard," Trevor calling after her. "Trevor I really must be off. It was a pleasure to see you as usual. Don't take any wooden nickels." She scurries off down the long, gray, endless hallway.

She returns to her own art studio cluttered with blood, dripping from a bucket near her grey wall. She has been dipping large oceanic sponges into buckets of blood, washing it over the wall. "Honey, when you go to the market, could you bring me back some fisheyes? I really need them for my latest experiment. "If you insist my Angel of light and darkness," disgruntled he exits the scene, a newspaper tucked and rolled under his arm. "Sheesh!" he mutters under his breath.

She sighs, putting her chin on her hand, staring at a canvas on the floor covered in blood-soaked sponges." I really must tell them at the meet what Trevor is up to, I'm sure they won't approve. But it is my obligation to keep them informed." Trevor is packing up crates with shredded paper, Styrofoam bubbles, hammering shut the top of the wooden containers. "Ouch!" as he hits his thumb.

Greta posts an invitation on his door in bright fuchsia. He takes his time finding it, then opens it after she has scurried away. "You are invited to a party at Factory Gallery next Saturday eve. Dress comfortably." Then Greta, one early Sunday morning pounding loudly with her fist on Trevor's studio door. "Let me in! It's time for your evaluation." It was only 9am. Most of the artists, forty in all were either asleep or in recovery for last night's parties. "It's time for me to take a look at what you are sending the Tate Gallery. I wanna make sure that ..." she scratches her mop of black, raven hair. To ... to ... to ... be sure it is your very, very best. Or they will surly annihilate you Trevor." Trevor laughs gaily, "It can't be that bad Greta. Have you had your breakfast? I have some English muffins here and café au lait." "I can assure you my dear, it is that bad? Why I must monitor everything carefully in accordance with the provisionary rules of the colony. If this is not a good match, then we will simply have to move you along to the other art colony where more is merrier. It is fundamental that you meet our specifications to qualify, to remain at this colony. Thank you for the café. It is scrumptious. Now to work. Let me see." She lies prone of his white canvas sofa with her feet up, entwined as she sips his offering. He waits petulantly as she passes her long, spindly hands through a gamut of black and white paintings, washes mostly, which he is preparing for this blue chip gallery in London town.

The works are large, stark and Expressionist with large brushstrokes of visceral energy thoughtfully simplified to be most effective. His influences were negligible, however Franz Klein came to mind. She sits curled up like a cat sipping pensively. He stands with a resolute grin in front of his best work of the season. "I hate this one!" She frowns. "What are you trying to say? It boggles my mind. What is this smudge over here? "She points out with verve and purpose.

Suddenly she takes an 18x24", throwing it on the ground, face down smashing the glass surface. "Hideous", she shrieks stomping her black boots around in circles. "It will never never do!" You must remember that the Gestapo will be at the opening night with shit eating grins on their faces. What does der Fuhrer sees this tripe?" "Bah humbug", he sits in his easy chair. "Who does they think they are." If they are hanging around London, so be it. Neville doesn't seem to care. He even gives Herr Hitler the benefit of the doubt. He seems to believe he's holding back a wave of Fascism." "Of course he is. it's obvious," her legs relaxed luxuriously on the canvas sofa. She is in her element.

The recumbent critic of All. The go-to for critiques and laughter. She awaits his come-on. She is hungry for his touch.

"I am so sick of my husband I can't even go there." Trevor laughs gamely. "I don't know what he's thinking of. I must have variety or die." She stirs her demitasse cup with a tiny coke spoon. Trevor glares now at his work." I know this one will be a success. I feel it in my bones." "Yes, my dear, it will be the premiere exhibition of the season. Everyone will attend. Goebbels, Goering, et al. I am certain of this." "Say, do you have any brandy? I am dying for a smoke too. In a minute I shall feel like ripping this thing off," as she pulls at her white chiffon blouson." Goebbels? Oh, that one! Just ignore him. He'll be a "Yes luv, come her and tickle my feet." She throws off her pointed Chinese slippers.

His neighbor, Anna could hear them screaming and howling for Hours. She rolls her eyes as she tries to paint her masterpiece on the dividing wall. After awhile a loud plop onto the cement floor. Anna assumes that one of them is sated.

BLUE CHIPPY

S aturday eve rolls around. Trevor has shipped his artwork to London for his prime, blue chip exhibition at Tate Gallery. There are kroner signs in his eyes of blue. When the reception finally rolls around, he is ecstatic. However he keeps his cool so as not to appear overanxious. "Never let them see you sweat", are his by-words.

He is so proud of himself that he dresses to the nines. He is wearing a semi-tux, with a fake t-shirt which in a painterly fashion resembles a tux and tie.

His coat has long tails. He struts his stuff around, "The Factory." He is grinning from ear to ear, sipping champagne by the gobful.

Greta greets him, decked out in a Balenciaga black, velvet from head to toe, a diamond brooch collecting the folds off the shoulder. Her bony elbows and shoulders are on full display revealing every wart and blemish, as Greta enters the main art gallery.

Vivaciously, she is toasting him with a champagne flute. The waiter carries a silver tray of Belgian chocolates. "Here's to happy times," she eyes him lasciviously, grinning sharply at him" "My you look the deb tonight, Trevor my dear!" spinning her web slowly, slowly, entangling, entrapping him as she shivers into a ball of confusion, becoming drunk about her new conquest.

"Thank god my Hubble's got taste. He fronted this whole thing. All for me, to the tune of fifty thousand kroner. I hope you like the orderves. They were flown in from Stuttgart just for laughs," Greta merrily.

She tosses her wavy tresses over her shoulder with flair. This dress is starting to slip off her shoulders like her demeanor. Drowning in pink, sparkling bubbles of effervescent dreaming; she trips over her long, black gown merrily giggling to jokes known only to her. Greta will feel this victory for many years of pained waiting, as Trevor runs after his male friends. He fancies a tight rump in the morning.

Enter the dragon, a tall, black, haired man with a black tux. He owns the joint lock, stock and barrel. His fingernails are painted five different lurex shades. He has dominion over all creatures in the gallery. Greta knows it and demurs to his verbal jousting with the artists. His favorite spot, besides of course, his bi adventures of all types. He has millions to play with from daddy. He lets them know it. He refuses to buy any artworks," It's really better if they beg me," wincing as he tugs at his bowtie. "I hate to say this but she's flat on her can again," whispering to his frowsy, Brazilian companion.

He just glares at her for a few seconds, then douses her with a glass of champagne, aiming for her brow. His companion reels in laughter. Greta remains lying there. "Thanks for the baptism, Clive. Really!' He saunters away; his Blondie girl tagging after.

Greta remains there smugly, face up, staring at a spider crossing the ceiling; the Arbitrator of taste for the entire Colony. The night wears on into the early morning hours as literally hundreds of culturally starved persons visit the gallery. Greta sidles up to a weary Trevor at daybreak, crashed out on the black, leather sofa.

"I have a perfect surprise just for you honey!", she smirks. "Come this way. Follow me!" She leads him up the back cement staircase, four flights a huge, empty art gallery, the door wide open. It's over thirty feet of white, stark, empty walls, a gray, concrete floor freshly cleaned. Damned expensive with no takers.

"Now we are going to play." As he steps into the gallery, he can't help but notice five, grey, metal buckets lined up in a row.

The first contains white feathers. Scratching his 4 o'clock fuzz, he surveys the scene. Suddenly she slams the door." We are alone now, just you and me!" She dances around him gaily. "You really do look so very handsome tonight. "She points to a simple wooden chair." Sit there bitte for my performance. "May I blindfold you? It's really better if I do that." He nods, placing his large hands on his thighs passively.

Within an instant she takes the bucket of feathers pouring them all over his head. "What did you feel?" she coyly asks giggling." Something soft, as woman's love,' he responds. The she takes a bucket of black, acrylic paint, thinned with turpentine. She pours the thick syrup all over his body. She laughs uncontrollably as it seeps into every crevice of his tuxedo. "Good Lord woman, what have you done?" he grimaces. "Why shouldn't a painter experience body painting?' When he attempts to stand up, he notices that she has roped him into the chair. "Now just a moment, we must let it dry!" she smirks. "Am I to become body art Greta?' Trevor puzzles. "It smells so bad. What is this?" "Now Trevor, you must play along." Must I? I think you've gone bonkers Greta.

"Just one more bucket should do the trick!" she grabs a bucket of blood, pouring it only below Trevor's belt. "Now you know how it feels to be woman, "Greta gravely. "Now look here, I've had quite enough of this!" "I am merely trying to educate you, you big lug!" she screeches in his ear, hovering over him like a crazy bird. "I think you'd better untie me, my dear," he struggles in the chair to loosen the rope ties. "Now for the piece de resistance," Greta takes her last bucket pouring piss all over the man. He cries out," Let me out of here, you sick witch!" "Not in your life! Not after what you did to me!' "You refused to even exhibit your art with me in 1932, if you recall correctly, and I resent that." "I never dreamed it was so important to you my dear. I would just like to leave." She sits next to him, her legs tightly crossed in a peach chiffon gown. "At this moment, Greta I plotting her next artistic move. Once again Trevor struggles to stand up. He then throws himself back onto the ground tied to the chair, in a vain attempt to break the wooden legs. "Oh Trevor, you look so funny!' laughing at him uproariously. Suddenly a small, reluctant knock on the door. "Honey is that you?" she searches the peephole with her small tightened, poker face. "It's only me, your faithful consort" Seth whispers. "What have you got going on in there, sweetheart?" The constant dupe, he caters to her every whim. "Oh nothing just a little experiment, I will see you downstairs. I am almost finished," gaily. "All right my love," Seth exits the scene, goes outside the huge arts building to smoke a Havana cigar, he has reserved just for the occasion. He props his left foot onto a stone on the ground surveying the stars above.

Greta removes a small penknife from the innumerable fold's in her skirt. She places it near Trevor's still blindfolded face. Now I am going to show you what Saint Jerome feels. You artists are supposed to be saints you know," placing the pen knife near his temple." But you're an artist too Greta," he feels the cold sharpness. "Well, I never fancied myself as much of a painter," she frowns. But you're a very successful one, I take it. With that all important show in London."

"Now this will only take a moment. You will feel nothing, then you will just pass out." "Whatever do you mean my dear?" Within several minutes, she has peeled back the skin off his brow. She thinks of Michelangelo's depiction of Saint Jerome in El Vaticano, as she performs her well-conceived plan. She is in an almost dreamlike state of consciousness. "There, that should do it. I have proven once and for all that men can't take pain." It's curious that after Trevor's shrieking, no one has come to his aid, in the vacuous art galleries. They must have emptied out with the arrival of dawn, like the Walls of Valhalla. She stares at Trevor, now passed out in the chair. She stomps her little foot. "Wake up, you must wake up! I'm not finished yet!" Greta is adamant.

She opens up the huge door, running to the freight elevator shaft, screeching for her husband Seth. "Seth, honey, you must come up her at once. Trevor won't move.'

This female seems barely human. She has cleverly fooled Jews, pretending always to be on their side. She calls on entities from a little black book. She claims to be an avid follower of the noted British, Satanist Aleister Crowley, quoting him verbatim at parties for negative attention, which she frequently receives. Unfortunately, she has called on so many entities of negative energy; they frequently consume her. This leaves leave her screeching, often for eight hour stretches, tearing at her black, raven tresses, cursing mankind. She is hospitalized after her neighbor's witness the horrors of the damned in their community. They cannot see her intent, which is obtaining her lifelong vendetta. She frequently roams the city late in the evening, after an extravagant gourmet supper at the Grand Hotel in the city.

She breaks into private apartments looting them, stealing identity papers for her prostitute companions. She claims to be saving them. She claims to her friends loudly, to have eliminated their roles. She stands proudly at Nazi meetings to say that she is cleaning up the neighborhood. Her party has given her a mission in life. She feels somehow vindicated every Thursday night at 8pm, when she boldly professes her efforts to pleas the Party membership. She is applauded with great fervor. It gives her a much needed sense of being part of something.

Her husband Seth is no angel. He owns five houses of prostitution in Berlin. He keeps the girls drugged, as well as hitting his wife with heroine frequently to 'keep her sweet' as he states calmly. Seth is usually the cool type until he gets riled up, then he hits the ceiling.

The artists somehow tolerate this behavior never questioning their intentions, until they are hit up themselves, which is often too late in this game. She loves to turn her husband's lovers into hookers, hitting them frequently with needles, dressing them up like pretty paper dolls; then dragging them to swanky nightclubs, selling them to businessmen after she has drenched them in cheap perfume. Greta likes to pour it over their heads; she calls it a baptism of desire. These rag dolls have had the best education money can buy. Their families are unaware of Greta's treatment of them. Of course, these artists are too afraid to tell, fearing censure and derision, or being monetarily cutoff from the family, due to family hypocrisy.

After a spin in his old car, Seth pistol whips these girls (artists) to keep them "on the up and up", he says." I rule my den", he states sullenly, putting his luger under his belt.

"NEMESIS"

Now Greta haunts this well-known art colony in Berlin as she has for thirty years. She experiences no censure from the artists, who take it as a matter of course that she is a freaky thing. They turn their heads, walking away, sometimes briskly. Unaware of her murders, performed frequently in ritualistic practices there on the property; the colony artists avoid the topic. Lying to themselves to seek solace, to just live with it.

One is a handsome friend, who reports her activities to the police. He warns artists off her. She has a date with this graphic artist making a distinct visitation, arguing loudly for all to hear.

There is a fervor in East Berlin among the theatrical set. Many theaters have censors who visit with notepads in hand, wearing spectacles during rehearsals of a new play. These Gestapo agents are headed by Joseph Goebbels, who is the Minister of German Culture and Propaganda. These agents have the goal to censor liberal playwrights; often disposing of their materials. The frequent book burning in both Vienna and Berlin has a huge impact on the arts and culture in Germany. Artists cringe at the sight of these uptight, note carrying bureaucrats, whose goal apparently is to expunge anything Non-Aryan from the theatre. Many playwrights are either imprisoned for obscenity, as defined by the Reichdom, or driven into oblivion by Gestapo agents. About seventy of these writer's commit suicide. They may have been brainwashed. They called this spirit of censorship and destruction, "The Mephisto." It is the spirit from the Mephisto waltz, a gloomy presence of death which haunts Germany.

This little devil is always the Prince of Lies. He embodies the spirit of; deception, slander, gossip, all to deceive the Germans into believing that murder, and torture of others will improve their lives.

The spirit of Mephisto roams the streets, spreading this new found illusion; of dreams, of acquiescence, power, idealism, perfection, an all-white society, purged by their peers, for all Germans. Germans feel empowered by these charismatic delusions of grandeur promoted as an opiate to the people. This becomes the pain killer which they swallow whole.

This spirit wanders the streets of Berlin in a blue haze, destroying with a swift hand, the freedom of these artists so hard won. It shatters like a crystal glass. This spirit of repression is so stringent, unforgiving and relentless. Many artists flee Germany in the thirties to seek artistic freedom in Eastern Europe. Cities there become Bohemia for them. They can now write whatever they are inspired to express, especially criticism of a Fascist regime, torture of civilians and the like. The Minister of Culture, Josef Goebbels, combined with the Gestapo have made a first move to strangle society. It is most effective amongst idealistic people who begin to question their work pitiably. They will become self- censoring, creating a world of namby- pamby PG rated nonsense suitable only for the under twelve set.

It is often thought that Adolf Hitler's psychology is the same. A closet, confined boy; boxed up in his own fantasy world unable to develop normally. During his childhood, he was often confined inside a wooden box, which was used to discipline him for several days at one time without food or sustenance. This sensorial deprivation created a monstrous vengeance. This distorted Hitler's views of love, forgiveness, compassion, and nurturing.

Compassion, he apparently did not experience from his drunken father. His seething hatred of others abounded later, when he was handed the keys to power in Berlin. Perhaps these dark mysteries of Hitler's childhood now suddenly surged to the forefront, as he attained power.

Adolph felt the need to regain his own personal power by punishing his strict disciplinary parents. He took it out particularly, towards elders in society, often ordering his men to shoot them, if they we're not laborers working round the clock.

He also had a ruthless agenda to eliminate a generation of questioners, who would remember the violent coup d'état.

At age twenty-one, on his birthday, Hitler had stormed Vienna with his troops, in the middle of the night. He placed a revolver to the head of President Dollfuss, blowing it to smithereens.

At exactly midnight, he had found President Dollfuss alone in his private study having a brandy. He rapidly dispensed with this head of government, who is vehemently opposed to the Aryan culture. Brown shirts are visiting Austria in droves in squad cars crossing over from Germany at the borders. The Viennese resent this intrusion into their nation. They empty huge trash cans onto the streets, shooting off their pistols into the air with abandon, screaming obscenities. The Fascist slogans, whitewashed on the grey stone walls of the city. The Viennese populace repels these Brown shirts who cross the border regularly into Vienna causing riots, overturning trash cans, burning refuse in the streets. The Viennese complain bitterly to the government headed by President Dollfuss. But a young upstart causes a coup d'état overnight.

Hitler choses to make a formal announcement at the Opera House in Vienna, behind a screen upstairs, high above the stage. A microphone is set up in place. As people dance to a favorite light opera, they hear a booming interruption. As the quests attempt to flee upon hearing the announcement on a loudspeaker, in the Grand Ballroom of the Vienna Opera House, the dancers instead freeze in fear. President Dollfuss is a well-loved leader. His assassination shocks this cultured society to the guilder steins.

Upon hearing that their country is now overrun with Nazis in a forced takeover, many Viennese attempt to flee the nation. However, the Nazi squadrons are strategically in place to fire upon the intelligentsia, as they depart the Opera House in hysteria. Outraged, the Viennese attempt to strike back at the deliberate overthrow of their nation's government by this twenty-one-year-old brute with a gang of toughs.

The Austrians hold the line against the Brown shirts, along the

Rhine for ten years, to prevent the Nazi insurgence into the country. They are completely opposed to Hitler and his rhetoric. Many Austrians perceive him as a madman already. His reputation has preceded him to their borders. They had fought along the borders of the Rhineland for long enough. Realizing the aggressive plans of this new leader and his slapdash government; they choose to fight him back. Thousands of locals at this Opera House are gunned down in the streets, as they fight the Brown shirts outside the Opera.

This throws many Austrians into a tumultuous dance with death. Many fear this forceful coup d'état will occur, but no one in Vienna foresees that this young tyrant will actually succeed by murder and mayhem. The night of Dollfuss' assassination, literally five-thousand Viennese are mowed down in the streets by force of arms. Stultified, many succumbed under this aggression to comply with this new provisional government from Germany.

Many Viennese- Austrians hate Hitler and his Brownshirts1 vehemently. They are fundamentally opposed to this new Third Reich. As such, they act out of self-preservation only to work within the strictures and confines of this regime. It is considered by some Austrians in 1938, an Act of God that the Austrians successfully expunge Hitler's base of power in their occupied nation first, before any other European Nation.

Finally, they are rid of this upstart, this madman bent of the total destruction of Western Europe. They replace him with a Catholic leader they trust. This finally produces peace and tranquility in Austria, before the final meltdown in Berlin with General Patton's forces at the helm. It takes nearly two decades to abolish this force of evil from Germany.

The Gestapo refuse repeatedly to honor the Geneva Convention by torturing officers who are held interminably in German built P.O.W camps.

The abject murder by the hundreds of captured political prisoners and Jews by Nazi machine guns is commonplace. These captured prisoners are never allowed a trial or even questioning. Escapees are usually shot on site; men, women and children are killed regularly in purges in the Jewish ghettos. It is so obvious Jews are forcibly moved to these barbed wire ghettos. They are being sequestered for political reasons. It leads to an early round up, to tag them with armbands, thereby separating all Jews from Aryans. These people, now forced under the gun, to wear armbands, which brand them as Jews, are destined for relocation to the German ghettos. Once there, they are sequestered behind a high wire fence.

Any other person who aids or abets them will be punished or killed in public view. Their leader is assassinated in the night, many shooting their way out. Bands of Brown shirts from Germany, shot thousands down in cold blood who oppose this coup d'état.

Many highly cultured intelligentsia of Austria are gunned down. They opposed the takeover by this young, ambitious Hitler at age twenty-one. On his birthday, Hitler had seized the nation of Austria with a handful of Extremist Terrorists.

BERRY-AU-BAC

It's midnight. A flight squadron has passed over Berry-Au-Bac, a small French village. It has been blitzed, pitted with potholes and leveled by Panzers squadrons of the Luftwaffe. The villagers, mostly trades people and farmers are devastated. Sanitation is now of the crudest kind. Roads on the cobbled Main Street are made of rough flint stones. Homes have maintained their rabbit hutches in the back. These poor villagers can sell rabbit skins in a pinch for a few centimes. The old men still maintain the beet fields of maroon, leafy, dark green. All the young men have been drafted and are away.

The "Marie' in the center of this village, is a particularly ugly building. It was probably built during the time of Louis Napoleon.

During these days of scarcity, French husbands, fathers, as well as "Le Vielle" field workers, manage to earn only fifty centimes per day (20 cents). They forage through fields, ravaged by the war, to glean crops near Rouen. There is a pioneer crop of U.S. airmen, stripped down to their waists, working in the open air.

They fell trees, building ramps and digging in the village. One of them is Aussie Mac, a wood carver from Melbourne. He is a cheerful, two-hundred pound, blonde guy with an infectious smile. His duties are to set up camp near the village center as soon as they can, to avoid excess carnage at the hands of the enemy. Soon the Panzers will approach bombing this region to smithereens. It will begin a 0:800 hours.

They have sequestered their planes nearby from the Luftwaffe. They have stashed their petrol, and bombs near a temporary headquarters.

There is a military road in Rheims-Loan, which is fronted by field of beets and corn. Miles and miles of yellow, and maroon patches from an aerial perspective entice flyers, to fly even lower to discern what lies below. It is one of the only ways out of the village for tanks and troops. Scrub brush is being used to camouflage the supplies near Berry-Au-Bac town center.

Aussie Mac is an officer in the bomb squad. He is red beet faced, cheerful, as well as a natural wood-craftsman. He does all the building ops for the squad. He wields an axe with great authority to fell trees. He has shaped many logs into ramps and bridges. At meal time, the men are given their ration of tinned bully beef, and a portion of biscuits. Dinner is served from a rickety portable kitchen, pulled down to the base each night in the back of a bus.

With any luck the men have their share of beef stew. The old portable stove is washed down with cheap red wine, the French call Pindar. It is not to everyone's taste, but it does the job of cutting the grease. Some wash it down themselves and even scrub themselves with it. It makes them smell like a fruitful harvest of grapes.

The first level operation is a high level reconnaissance over the frontier. Formations fly at 20,000 feet. They are met with heavy antiaircraft fire. However, they manage to bring back valuable photos of the terrain and nearby Panzers.

The Allies are smoking cigarettes in the camp awaiting the new days ops. It is deadly quiet, due to their newfound proximity to a Panzer troop.

Aussie Mac is relaxing on a cot, for the evening, chewing tobacco. He regales the men with his Australian humor. The troops look disillusioned, untidy, ill-clad, uninterested in the future. It is cause for concern with Aussie Mac. They are bored reserves, awaiting action to prove themselves. They have held this position at Berry Au Bac for three months now. To drum up some hope, air-gunner Roberts has scrounged some eggs, vegetables, even coffee grounds from nearby fields. Two-Ton, the Wing Commander arrives late. His reconnaissance plane has had a false landing nearby.

In the dug outs filled with mud, there is a chimney belching smoke

from the nearby cave dwellers as well. Men are squirreled away everywhere within sight of each other. The dawn awaits them.

The officers have set up camp at the Chateau at Guignicourt, near
the banks of the River Aisne. It is proudly owned by the Marquise de
Nazelle, a charming, white-haired, delicate woman, with six sons and
one daughter, all underage. She is anxious to protect them from the
encroaching furor. She has welcomed these American Officers with
champagne and orderves, a gourmet meal and polite conversation. The
Americans know little French as they strain to understand her, but are
appreciative of the hospitality. A butler serves them all the meals, except
breakfast which is taken impromptu in the kitchen quarters, smorgas-
bord style. There is also a British Governess for the children. Dinner is
always served at a round table vivaciously with élan.

The British troops are eating club and mess hall style, a decided
contrast. Under the village cobblestones lie the Champagne Caves, where
many miles of tunnel run underground below the outskirts of this city.
The champagne grapes are still collected seasonally in these underground
passageways. The sweet, baby grapes make the finest champagne. Many
restaurateurs have underground tunnels and caves for storage of vintage
wines. Wines must be kept cold after bottling. Many Allied troops also
walk through these passageways.

As the men familiarize themselves with these caves, Aussie Mac
formulates a scheme. He regards all the troop as his brothers and now
begins to worry about the lassitude of this war. It begins to infuriate
the soldiers, standing around the following day while their buddies are
in battle. None are determined to fight, but will fight their damnedest
when given the chance.

Along the Rhine River between Austria and Germany is the Siegfried
line, an imaginary boundary has been fortified since 1932. There is a
watch constantly along the Rhine, for encroaching Brown shirts by the
Austrian Guard. The Austrians are loathe that these men would ever
cross into Austria. President Dollfuss has made it crystal clear that the
German Reich forces are unwelcome there. This watch is maintained

twenty-four hours a day, until finally Hitler and his men sneak into Vienna murdering hundreds in their wake.

It's dawn near the encampment. The men, sprawled out on cots are awakened by the sounds of Panzers, flying overhead. It jolts them out of their somnambulant sleep into quick action. These Panzers are swiping low along the border region of Northern France. They are flying down enough to take potshots with their machine guns at the encampment. A German Reconnaissance plane has discovered it during the night.

Corporal Downey immediately gives orders to evacuate the main camp. The artillery is manned with lightning speed. The gunnery officer scrambles to his machine gun. Machine gunners grab hold of their arms, aiming toward the skyline. They knock out one plane after the other. The debris falls nearby creating confusion, smoke, plus a wily fire which encompasses them all. With the smoke pouring through the area; the soldiers hit the dirt.

Some crawl away to a patch outside Lausanne which is free air space. One of the men grabs a red flag warning sign to signal for cover. However, with no Allied forces flying overhead there is little hope of backup anytime soon. The Corporal signals some of the men to head for the champagne tunnels. He knows he may lose half of his platoon in a New York minute. Some go underground, dragging the wounded to safety. Then they return to ground level quickly as the Panzers return with another blow. Suffering severe casualties; many are falling. It's effecting their morale as they muster up more courage to face the airstrike again. Surely now they can eliminate their foes before during a third go round. Aussie Mac has been hit on his thigh. He leans hard on a machine gun to stabilize his movements. He aims dead on, hitting a Panzer airmen square in the engine, exploding an aircraft which sails downward into a scorching blaze of fire and rubble.

Aussie Mac struggles with a tourniquet of torn t-shirt wound round his leg awkwardly to stop the flow of blood. One of his buddies grab his arm, moving him toward the tunnels. He is hit again in the backside, falling to his knees. His buddy carries him into the tunnel with every breath he has in him. He may survive. With all the noise and confusion several, men are hit falling to the cold, cold ground. Corporal Downey has lost fifteen fighting men in one hour. They now are moving as fast as possible through the underground maze to the other portion of Berry Au Bac. Some French villagers meet them inside the far reaching tunnel. They have some wine to kill the pain. Several scream out.

Aussie Mac squirms on a cot placed on the ground. He fears that he might lose his leg. The men have to abandon him for hours, while they revert to their former position to carry wounded and maintain artillery fire at the German squadron. The body count is devastating for this platoon. In the space of two hours, one third of their fighting regiment is demolished by the surprise attack. Corporal Downey signals for reinforcements, but there are none in the region. Desperate, he calls for air cover on a walkie-talkie. The sound breaks up continually, but he gets through a request. There is no time to lose. They retreat underground as Panzers keep returning, blowing up their ammo supply dump in the distance. Several radio men are struggling now with walkie-talkies for air support but no man comes.

A gunnery officer finally levels a Panzer, which nosedives into the area. Corporal Downey makes the decision for the troops to retreat underground. He has lost too many men. They remain there overnight nursing the wounded, praying for cloud cover or rain to evacuate to another location. With no ammo supplies or backup, it sets back all the best laid plans. They await the dawn.

Corporal Downey has given orders to relocated to the village of Berry Au Bac. The villagers are sad at the site of the wounded Allied forces returning to the town for some much needed assistance. The villages have also experienced casualties and damages to their thatched roofs. Many farms are demolished by the airstrike. These troops are welcomed into several farmhouses, by local French women who tend the wounded. Aussie Mac has survived so far, but is in unstable condition. Plans to regroup are imminent. They can't afford another airstrike.

Inside the Citadel there exists a large group of Secret Service agents, otherwise known as Black shirts, who did the bidding of Heinrich Himmler to the "T". Himmler has discovered an assassination plots to kill Hitler, hidden in a bureau, chock full of drawers. His rage is so forceful that he grabs a small envelope, pinned to a mahogany panel; stomps his foot loudly while screaming at an attendant. He is literally foaming at the mouth, which causes his attendant to be startled. The man straddles Hitler in his efforts to protect him. Hitler screams, "Get ahold of yourself man." Hitler begins twirling around in his desk chair like a small child, twirling and twirling, laughing and laughing. His attendant scratches his chin puzzled by this peculiar reaction to a death plot. It occurs to him that his leader has become increasingly mad. The attendant moves to the window. After a moment he stands to fling the drapes open, the attendant gazes out the window, his arm on the sill, his head leaned into his arm." What can I do?" he asks. Hitler enraged at his perceived incompetence; gives the guard at the door orders to kill him on the spot. The henchmen outside the door peers inside. He sees his leader wiping foam and spit from his mouth.

Hitler takes his Dutch assistant outside several paces, then puts a gun to his head execution style, making him kneel and beg. He cocks the trigger, but this gun is not loaded. He returns to his study, pulling the desk top drawer open where he finds cartridges. He then attempts, fumbling them angrily into his luger.

As he attempts to load the gun the Black shirt outside perceived Hitler's incompetence. The Dutchman remains kneeling with his eyes closed. The other black shirt in the room finally fires his own gun at the Dutchman, spattering blood all over the wallpaper. The Dutchman falls over. Hitler sits back in his desk chair twirling his thumbs and states flatly," I am sorry I killed someone again, "to his staff. The guard blurts out, "Well actually mien heir …" then he catches himself," Heil Hitler, "retreating outside to guard the entrance again. The bloodstains remained on the wallpaper for years. They cannot be expunged.

The story gets around town. The Dutch settlers are enraged. Many Dutch settlers are opposed to Hitler's stance. They migrate to South Africa. Hitler refers to them as White Niggers." Well if you don't do what I tell you, you can tend the White niggers in the South, "he screams at his minions. He will dismiss many Dutch this way. A colony of over fifty thousand émigrés from the war settle there, to escape the inane policies of Hitler. Most Dutch completely oppose this Reich and its agenda. The memory of this clerk was told so many times, it became part of Dutch culture.

It was a constant reminder that the never-ending cycle of violence has begun again in Germany. Like the spinning clock, a circular miniature presents a soldier, then a Swiss Miss chasing their fate in circles.

LAUSANNE

In Southern Italy, a troop of Black shirts storm a palace in the country-side. Several Brown shirts take the daughter of the owner of this estate, a young girl on nineteen, with dark black, wavy, tresses aside. They scold her sharply for allowing Allied soldiers to be stationed inside their home. Then all the girls present are forced, under the gun, to cook, clean and wait on these German troops hand and foot. The harsh treatment of these women remain in their psyche, giving over to an interminable rage. Enforced servitude being similar to enslavement.

One of the girls is stripped outside of the bunker, to show the field workers that the Reich is in charge of their village. The campesinos in the fields look away from the girl, knowing full well that this donna is fated for a horrible death. She is then pushed over the metal railings to her death one hundred feet down.

Later that evening some of the campesinos return to bury her secretly, carrying a few lanterns. To avoid further atrocities they dig one entire feet down raking the light sand over this Madonna.

Later after a few weeks the troop has recovered from the attack. One of the Officer, proud of his German American background reports to the tent where Corporal Downey is working to volunteer for an assigned duty. Werner salutes Corporal Downey." At ease, Werner you strike me as a competent man. What can I do for you this morning?" "Sir, request permission to ferret out the orphans near Lausanne during the night raid." "That operation would be too dangerous. It would involve too many men. Nix on that for security reasons." 'We would have to move them out as is convenient during the day.' "As you say sir, but I think

that will take too long to be effective sir." "Werner you are dismissed.'
"Yes sir," Werner leaves downhearted, saluting.

Later that same day, while canvasing the area near Lausanne a small
boy about nine runs along the side as the troopers panic while a German
MIG runs a line along the roadway. The gunfire nearly kills the child,
causing Werner to scoop him under his arm quickly and duck and roll.

Werner is keeping the child underneath him. "You're a real pain kid."
"Como? Rene responds. "Oh one of those French brats heh." "Okay,
okay, he shakes the kid standing him up, Via con Dios." "Como?" Rene
responds politely. The other soldier motions him to run off into the
shrubs. He scampers away. "That was Spanish, you idiot!" Buddy replies.
"That kid is French, Werner." "Okay fine," Werner falls over wounded.
He clenches at his right side. It is bleeding heavily. Buddy drags him off,
shaking his head.

That evening Werner is in the infirmary, his side wrapped up in gauze.
The Doc approaches him with a clipboard and pen. "That's quit a stunt
you pulled today. But you'll make it if you rest awhile. We have determined
not to send you him just yet." "Okay doc," Next time you might not be so
lucky. By the way the kid survived. He is the barkeep's son. Why don't you
go by there when you're up an about?" "Sure will. But I think the kid only
speaks French. "A pretty French nurse overhears them and walks over to
him." I vill assist this monsieur.' She sits down at the end of the bed with a
chalkboard. French lessons are in the offing. He smiles wanly.'Maintenant,
les verbes: Je suis, Ta a, Nous Sommes, Vous etes." "Sheesh", Werner rolls
his eyes to heaven. 'Je suis", she repeats' as …"

In a few days he is on a crutch hobbling into the cantina with his mates.
There are three of them in fresh uniforms. "Set him up Joe," Paul says his
eyes gleaming. "Paul is a tall drink of water with deep brown eyes. "The
first rounds on me", Werner stands up to the barkeep. "Where's that little
kid of yours?' "Lui e las bas," pointing to him, washing dishes in the back
room. "Merci bien pour mon garcon monsieur.' "De rien", Werner smiles.

"See I learned some French from that pretty nurse, and a few other
things." The lads have a laugh. "Like what Werner? Like what other
things? "She sure has a cute derriere. I like the way she wiggles." "Oh

yeah, here's to its wiggle!" They lift three beer glasses. "That wiggle is mon fille!" the bartender spits at him." "D'accord, ton fille?" "Oui mon fille," he wipes down the bar. Elle a un bon travail avec le docteur la," "Oh boy, Werner, say something quick," Paul interjects. "Ah, maybe I'll take her back to America with me. "Oh no, Elle e las bas" pointing his finger to the air," Avec le docteur" decidedly.

'What the Sam Hill is he saying anyhow? "Bo puzzled. "Well it seems that nurse is his daughter and he won't part with her knowhow Bo, "smiles Paul.' "Well that's a shame. She's a pretty little filly, "Bo grinning from ear to ear. I might fancy a look see meself. With that ass, I'll bet she's ripe for the taking, eh buddy?" His buddy scratches the back of his neck," Oh for Christssake!"

"Not on your life knit-wit. Why your too crude a man for that mademoiselle. "Is that so Werner?" Bo hauls off and hits Werner on the chin. He stumbles forward with a stupid expression on his face. Paul says, 'Hey, what did you do that for you knucklehead? 'to Bo, "Can't you see the man's on a crutch? "Oh yeah, let me help you up Werner, "He fakes him out dropping him onto the table.

Bo takes no prisoners. He's from the deep South, near Point Du Lupe. Werner lies sprawled on top of the table. The child runs out from behind the bar to aid him. He stands there his mouth gaping. Werner, 'I'm okay kid," Werner, "Hand me my crutch kid." Rene finds his crutch on the ground, handing it to him readily. Bo drowns him in beer. "You have been baptized, Kraut." "You know those are fighting words, Bo. I think enough is assez bien or something along those lines," Paul dismisses the two to talk to a pretty barmaid." "Yeah, there are cheap tarts and there are sweethearts 'Werner muses staring at the barmaid. You know, "Paul is smarter than the average Bear, "observes Bo to the recalcitrant Werner. The night wears on.

At dawn Paul is escorting the barmaid to her little thatched roof Maison with a kiss on the cheek.

General Montgomery walks down the red marble hallway along the side of Saint Peter's Basilica in Rome, headed toward the office of

Cardinal Rosso. He is with his right hand man. He doffs his cap as a Swiss Guard opens the glass doors for him, saluting him.

As the General strides in; he spies out of the corner of his eye, a German Gestapo agent in full, black regalia, carrying a luger, his breast decorated with an iron cross and several ribbons. This Black shirted soldier is seated in a high backed, gold, gilded, chair covers in rich tapestry. He glares right back at Montgomery. General Montgomery walks over to him. He attempts conversation. The German Gestapo agent lifts up his cup of coffee, shakes his head and replies," Nien.""Very well." Montgomery is miffed at the rude manner of this man." We may be at war but we could at least be civilized," Montgomery pointedly, "Ve vill be civilized when the war is over and you are eating from our hands mien Herr," drinking this coffee coolly.

Montgomery take this seat near the door, 'Very well, "he stares blankly into space. "General Patton and I will be at your front door before you know it," steely eyed. There is palpable tension in the room. The Gestapo agent stands up, he leans on the corner of a gilded desktop, "I hear your General Patton got lost in a sandstorm near Marrakech and villa not be joining us this evening."

"Not at all, he's anxious to meet you, perhaps tomorrow afternoon. "As it happens, I have an engagement with the Cardinal. It concerns some missing prisoners of the Jewish variety, some five hundred." "You have misplaced that many mien Herr? Montgomery is now in his element. "Ve think ve vill have to discipline these priests."

"That so? "he faces off with him. As he does so a priest walks into the room gravely, "The Cardinal vill see you now General Rickover". He strides ahead into the antechamber. The gold, gilded doors close.

"That man is General Rickover? I thought he was a common Lieutenant, "Montgomery scoffs to his man on the right.

Hours pass, General Montgomery is pacing the floor. Finally General Rickover strides out the door with a priest in tow behind him. "We will try to take care of that for you as soon as humanly possible General, "Father Uccello." Heil Hitler, "General Rickover salutes the air. Montgomery passes him with steely eyes glaring once again at his face.

The Italian government is now being leaned on by General Montgomery. They need Visas and quickly for one hundred small émigrés in Roma. The Cardinal seems relieved to see him. General Montgomery exits with a pleased look on his face. Under his arm he carries a satchel of documents.

It's 1935, France has been stormed and captured by the Nazis after a long and bitter struggle. Hitler's cronies are striding purposefully down the Champs Elysee. It is late evening. Hitler stares at Himmler pointing out that," I am the king of all I survey," with his trusted riding crop. Then suddenly he swats Himmler who is nonreactive. "Yes, mien Fuhrer," he blurts out, feeling this bum.

"It has always been my fondest wish to raid the Louvre of it's treasures. Perhaps you would like to join me on this escapade?" Hitler has a gleam in his eye. "Yabull mien Fuhrer," Himmler clicks his heels together in accordance. "We will pressure the French government first, later when they are shivering; we will surround the Louvre with two regiments relieving them of their masterpieces. It will be a magnificent accomplishment." "You are so right to say this, mien Fuhrer." "Are you correcting me?" Hitler becomes enraged. "Nien mien Fuhrer, a slip of the tongue," stuttering. Himmler frequently stutters when angry. As Hitler promenades down the Champs Elysee with Himmler to his left, he mumbles to himself. Himmler observes this game.

Himmler never forgets this treatment holding a resentful rancor in his heart for years. He later chronicles it in a novel which is never published.

Himmler write and writes reams of paper in order to publish his memoirs, but the public will never have accepted it after the close of the war. So it remains there in piles and piles of papers on his desk for years. Eventually the dust settles on it. He remained alive for thirty years in the penitentiary outside Berlin itself. His war crimes were so pervasive and unrelenting; The Hague tribunal sentenced him to five life sentences. There he remained writing his stories in a prison cell.

Hitler had a taste for fine Belgian chocolates which he dunked into his coffee cup savoring the flavor. He knew it went to his waistline and being a proud narcissist he began to dance around the room every time he had chocolate with any willing female in the room for hours twirling them about. Some consider this charming but the vast majority of these frauliens were sanguine.

Hitler was so distracted from his command they questioned his resolve, especially his guards who chuckled under their breath as he twirled round these blonde bombshells with glee. Hitler had a compulsion to read pornography under his desk. He began to fantasize about an actress named Eva Braun, who pictured herself in the nude in skin mags. After arranging a meeting, she was literally dragged in from of him made to lie down as Hitler rolled her up in a carpet with his feet and deposited her outside the door That was their first meeting in his office in Berlin. Eva knew that they had smooch power she either cooperated or had her pretty head copped off which was his predilection for what he called, 'bad girls.' He numbered his lovers on his right hand. Very few damsels would even touch him He smelled of iodine which he used frequently on his rear end to assuage an old wound. He had received the wound as a child from his father.

His father played very rough games with him. He hated his father with such severity his face would light up, as his eyes bugged out. "I hated the old man "he would repeat laughing sometimes to himself. He also hated sexual relations inventing all kinds of tortuous activity for Eva Braun to perform for him or on him including pissing on his head as he lay down in front of her. Perhaps he thought he deserved it.

Eva Braun made several films with Otto Preminger as the Director. He was considered one of the most notorious Directors in Germany. He refused to listen often to the Gestapo's dictates enraged a them, carrying a full buggy whip, which he would snap at them. They would hop amazed at his arrogance. He was never arrested for his mimicry of der Fuhrer.

Otto made an arrangement with several US agents to get out of Germany, as the walls went tumbling down like Jericho. In the amidst of the war, Otto Preminger immigrated to America. It saved his career from ruin by the SS guard, who monitored him frequently.

Otto Preminger became a premiere filmmaker in Hollywood, frequently working at MGM studios. He befriended many American actors including Frank Sinatra, who starred with Kim Novak as the junkie in "The Man With the Golden Arm," many critics considered this film Preminger's, masterpiece. Pauline Kael, the famous New York critic praised his insight and realistic depiction of drug addiction.

Winston Churchill is preparing a speech alone in his study, at his oak and marble desktop. He works into the early dawn. The next day as he walks into the antechamber of the House of Lords, he pauses awhile to speak with the Press Secretary, Colville. "What will you speak to this morning Prime Minister?" "I have only on purpose, the destruction of Hitler", he explains to Mr. Colville hurriedly on his way inside the Grand Hall. "And my life is much simplified thereby. If Hitler invaded Hell, I would make at least a favorable reference to the devil himself in the House of Commons." "Your speech appears to be full of passion as usual Prime Minister his assistant remarks.

"Can you doubt what our policy will be? We are resolved to destroy Hitler, and every vestige of the Nazi regime. From this nothing will turn us-nothing. Any minor state who fights against Nazi Dom will have our aid. It follows therefore that we will give whatever help or aid we can to Russia and the Russian people. "How did you arrive at aiding Stalin sir? 'Colville."

The struggle between Nazism and Communism is a case of dog eat dog." "There was a recent Papal encyclical sir, which states that Communism is intrinsically wrong and that no Christian civilization may give it assistance or any understanding whatsoever, "Colville reads from his notepad on the run alongside Churchill. "Is there anything you want to tell Stalin Prime Minister?" "Tell him, tell him Churchill said, tell him, that he can depend on us. Goodbye and God bless you Harry." Churchill enters a black limousine in the pouring rain of London town.

It's 8pm, Saturday evening, in Harlem. FDR is entering the Grand Ballroom with its gilded, Art Deco mirrored doors, it's white linen tablecloths with marbled, walnut tables, in Manhattan. He was enjoying a rare moment of peace; a concert with Eleanor. They are dressed to the nines. Eleanor is wearing a beaded chiffon gown. As he doffs his top hat, with a black, flowing cape; he hands his gold-tipped cane to the hat check girl. A messenger in a bellman's uniform, runs up to him rapidly. He tucks a crucial note into his hand. "Read this sir, it's urgent." "I certainly will, good sir." He gazes at the note; taking out his spectacles. It reads, "Hitler has invaded Russia." FDR runs into a telephone booth quickly, in the hallway of the theatre. "I insist on being taken to England at this time, to confer with the Prime Minister," to his secretary. She is awakened with a start at midnight by FDR. She sleepily sleepily puts on her glasses, searching blindly in the dark for her notebook."

"But you're ill sir, the doctor said you should not travel for awhile." "The doctor be hanged. I must speak with Churchill. FDR informs his colleagues immediately, with swift resolution, that "Churchill is the best man England has to offer." "We will investigate this new paradigm, set up by Hitler in this Russian invasion forthwith. "Bluntly, he hangs up the phone, closing the louvered glass door of the phone booth. He then proceeds with Eleanor to the balcony, on the fourth etiage, where the usher escorts them to their box seats above. He stands to wave, faking merriment, to the crowd. A panning spotlight hits his face from the stage, gamely smiling with a pained brow.

Back in Berlin, the self-appointed Chancellor is in his element; kicking at his desk, twirling his chair around like a small girl. "We expect to defeat Russia in just two months. They are weak at the knees, they have no fortresses, no real armaments. We can seize their troops in a flash." He pounds his desk with a fury, glaring at several Black shirts in assistance. His mahogany desk thunders with his pounding. The Black shirts around him are in accord with his pronouncements.

It is now 12:40 am, bombs begin to fall hard upon; Brussels, Amsterdam, Rotterdam, the low countries as well as France. In dozens of European villages, fire illuminates the sky.

Many Dutch clog the roads attempting to escape the city center of Holland with anything they can carry on their backs in muslin bags and old suitcases. In Amsterdam the roads are completely jammed. Bombs continue to fall on Dunkirk, Calais, and Metz in France.

Parachute troops are dropping to seize Dutch and Belgian airports quickly. The Governor of Luxembourg flees to France. Ambassador William Bullitt, confirms that the Germans has launched violent attacks on a half dozen French military bases. Bombs have fallen on the main railway between Paris and the border region.

It is Spring of 1940, the United States possesses almost no munitions at all. The British lack a developed Naval fleet for combat and have practically no Destroyers, aircraft carriers, or land craft ships. Winston Churchill has pleaded repeatedly with the House of Commons, the House of Lords and Elizabeth the Queen for such things. Unprepared for any real confrontation these leaders have now to approach their respective Parliaments and Senates for real preparation, for an all-out war.

While Berlin is burgeoning with troops and ulterior motives, the Third regiment is busy with the evacuation. A short term plan has been set up with the schools in London to receive incoming refugees.

There, they would be detained for at least six weeks, as part of their migration to either the United States or English families who will host them.

Corporal Downey is encouraged when he receives another wire from General Eisenhower, while stationed near the Vatican. It contains pertinent information which guides him through the logistical maneuvers of the operation Blackfoot scheduled to go down immediately. He quickly relays the info to his men around Rome.

They have to move quickly, Himmler's Left Guard are closing in for the kill. Hitler has already disseminated his seven percent solution in a fit of rage near the closing of the war. Hitler is pronouncing on National television in Germany and in parts of Austria that the plans to eliminate all non-white children, as part of his "general cleansing." The German people appear to accept this passively. Many children are being rounded up with huge butterfly nets, a contraption of Hitler himself, and thrown in gullies around the city, where helplessly they attempt to crawl out. These little ones are between four and ten years of age.

They grasp at straws; trying to jump out of these crevices. There are deep pits around Berlin and outlying regions. Stark cries are heard everywhere in the city. The citizens stay inside while this goes on; not daring to question or even challenge any of these atrocities. Many perish due to lack of food and water. They are simply left there to die. News of this quickly spreads like a gasoline fire, to France and England. The British are so appalled; they immediately send convoys of soldiers. They have no recourse but to send them through London, in the Tube.

Prime Minister Churchill announces via radio that "This will be our finest hour," to all and sundry, whose ears are glued to the Victrola's. The movement has begun to liberate these children, regardless of consequences. The seven percent solution, a brainchild of Heinrich Himmler and Hitler is in force. Thousands begun to be rounded up, torn from their domiciles and schools. They are not told where they are going. Some of the Brown shirts even get involved throwing curses at these young children loudly. They have been trained to insult and degrade others in school under Hitler's regime.

Before too long a convoy of children is flying through the city to Kindergarten for Kinder-sport. These orphans of the storm are then beaten by the other children, Aryans or course, some spat on and forced to disrobe. Then some are burned at the stake. The children in Brown shirts make a circle around the trees while they burn, chanting obscenities which were taught to them by the Gestapo. Corporal Al Downey witnesses all these things before the camp is liberated by Allies. Before long, the little children lay dead on the ground.

Again, these Brown shirted kinder have been taught to urinate on the dead. They leave these children lying there without burial procedures. The stench is so horrible that some of these German children pinch their noses. Some of the girls pass out.

The Kinder-sport is not over yet. The children have even been taught to yank out the fillings of the dead children for gold and silver. They collect the filings in brown paper bags which they give to their Commandant. He even counts them and awards prizes to them with yellow ribbons. This goes on for hours, as hundreds of children are brought into Kindergarten in convoys.

It was only then after accurate observations and films of these atrocities, that the Allied forces could move in to arrest the perpetrators of these inhuman acts towards children. It was at this juncture that the Allies began to drop bombs all over the place. They attempted to free the children from the internment camp called "Kindergarten," but it was difficult to get to them. Also, they were so inculcated by Hitlerian philosophy, the Gestapo had brainwashed these small youngsters to main and kill their peers. If they refused to cooperate, even when their little lives were threatened. When offered chocolate bars in an effort to evacuate them, they would spit them into the faces of the soldiers. The kinder sport had gone on for hours before the

Allies could locate the encampments. They were often in the countryside around Berlin. They were frequented by the Gestapo who trained these children to maim and kill for them. Anyone who was back was eliminated first, then yellow, then brown. It was so organized; it seemed like a weird dream. Even now Corporal Downey and others who attempted to liberate the kinder camps can't grasp it. How is such a thing possible? The brainwashing of these kinder was so thorough that they acted as one. It was a collective consciousness of brutality with a rewards system built in. The brainwashing of these kinder was all pervasive.

They air lifts managed to free up around two thousand children in the course of one day. Many storm troopers were also sent in from General Patton's army. They witnessed the most horrible, indescribable, atrocities that they were stymied by what the kinder where capable of doing to other children. Many of these orphans and children of color perished in the melee. However, with diligent rescue teams they did manage to save hundreds of lives that day. This purge went on for seven days, unrelenting under Hitler's tutelage. He saw to it that they were rewarded for brutal acts with medals as they gave him a salute. Many of those children are around today in West Germany, a haven for kinder from those days. Cologne is full of them.

KINDERCAMP

After the deluge of U.S. bombers managed to deploy, many of the Reichdom's military might was swayed completely. There now was an opportunity to alleviate the horrors set in motion by this regime.

Allies poured in from all sides of Germany. They surrounded Hitler in his bunker. He drank hemlock from a small vial he carried in his pocket thereby committing self-murder. The Bunk where he worked was ordered destroyed by his own men. As it burned the Allies stood in wonder ta this retreat. When all was said and done the charred bones revealed that Hitler was burned beyond all recognition. His jawbone, one of the few artifacts found in the rubble was identified by the DNA which Hitler has so jealously guarded in frozen tubes for reproductive measures. This was the first sperm bank ever created in 1932 near Warsaw. The remains of Hitler were never discovered due to Funeral pyre created by the Nazi's.

His scientist's in a grizzly experiment, had tried to prove, however mistakenly, that Hitler's frozen sperm would regenerate. It was a crude science in 1932, which bilked millions of dollars from vulnerable clients. The jawbone found inside the bunker near Rouen was identified by DNA evidence beyond a shadow of a doubt as that of Adolf Hitler's'. He had perished by his own hand to avoid capture. Josef Goebbels had hidden his six children down below in a bunker in the heart of Berlin. He gave his wife Katrina, a dram of hemlock to pour down the throats of each and every one of his children. They were all under the age on nine years. They drank it. Then Goebbels strode outside the bunker, which was below ground level. He regarded the entire building carefully. It had been shelled. He then chose to confront General Patton and his men outside, surprisingly by placing a gun to his temple and firing, one single shot. Al watched with General Patton in disbelief as he fell to the ground shattered like a lump of clay. Goebbels' blood spurted everywhere. Al watched in amazement as Patton simply kicked the lifeless body of Goebbels to make sure that he was really dead. Then Patton gave the signal to move along, leaving the lifeless body in the rubble.

It was the end of an Epoch; "the war to end all wars." Weary troops slowly wended their way back to their home countries with will to spare. They believed that they had rid the world of a real and present danger to democracy and peace. No one then would have ever thought that mankind would embrace such hedonistic racism and destruction again. The Allies were free of the curse of Fascism and Oppression. They could now breathe free in a land of milk and honey which promised them re-generation, love and valor. People really believed that it was all over. Back in Manhattan a ticker tape parade of gleaming rainbow colors fell softly on the returning veterans many of whom were driven in Oldsmobile's through the streets of Broadway to 47th Street. It was a moment of glory to be welcomed warmly by the citizens of New York City. It meant a lot to these returning warriors that we they did was accepted, honored and appreciated for decades to come. Eight million people had perished in this war. Many émigrés now graced the streets of New York with hope, and a vision and determination that this would never happen again.

BIBLIOGRAPHY

Maria Downey
January 28,2019

1. "Dietrich & Riefenstahl", by Karin Wieland, pub. by Liveright Pub. Assoc., NY, London ISBN 978-0-87140-336-0 2. "Best American Screenplays", edited by Sam Thomas, forward by Frank Capra, Crown Pub. Inc., NY @ 1986 3. "All Quiet on the Western Front", Abbott Version Universal Pictures,1930by William Banewell, Albert Krapps, George Abbott- final revision.Nov.11,1929 4. "Winds of War," by Herman Wouk, pub Crown Books,1941 5." Hangmen Also Die", film, Directed by Fritz Lang 6. "A Visual History of Weimar Films" 1918-1933, by Hans Helmut, pub. Thames & Hudson, ISBN 978-0-500-51689-8 7." Germans, Propaganda & Total War," by David Welch, pub. Rutgers University Press, New Brunswick, NJ ISBN 0-8135-2798-8 8." The Great Escape,' The Mirsch Co. Inc., Paramount 1041 Formosa Drive, Hollywood, 1962 9." The Great Inquisitor," play, by Fyodor Dostoyevsky excerpt from The Brothers Karamazov at The Valley Center Theatre, Sherman Oaks,2005 10." Europa, Europa", by Agnieszka Holland, Orion Pictures,1991 11. "Dr. Strangelove," by Stanley Kubrick, Columbia Tri-Star,1966

12. "The Last Lion," by William Manchester 13. "The Gathering Storm Vol. I & II," by Winston Churchill London 14." The Force of Destiny "by Chris Duggan, pub. Houghton Mifflin, NY, 2008 15." The Rise and Fall of the Third Reich", by William Shirer, (the unabridged version), pub. Eaton press,1936 16." One of Our Pilots is Safe", by William Simpson, pub.

Harper & Brothers, NY/London 1943 ISBN D811 SG10 18. "No Ordinary Time," by Doris Kearns Goodwin, Simon and Schuster paperbacks,1994.

ISBN 978-0-684-80448-4

19." Bertolt Brecht, on Film & Radio" written by Bertolt Brecht

by Marc Silberman (translator) pub. by Methuen 2000, London,1988

Press 1913-1956 ISBN 0-413-72500-6 20. "A Visual History of Weimar Film 1918-1933," by Hans Helmut, pub. Thames and Hudson ISBN 978-0-500-51689-8 2013 21." All Quiet on the Western Front ", written by Lewis Banewell & Alfred Knapp Nov.11,1929/ Directed by Lewis Milestone, released 24/Aug.19305 22." The Arrogance of Power,' by Anthony Summers,

ISBN 0-670-07151-6 23. "The Years of LBJ," by Robert A. Caro,

ISBN 0-394-52835-2 pub. Alfred Knopf, NYC 1990 24. "True Compass," by Edward M. Kennedy

ISBN 978-0-446-53925 25. "Vermeer" by Pierre Cabanne,2004, pub. Editions Terrail

ISBN 2-87939-2772 printed in Italy 26. "Berlin-Mendelson"-Erich #1590595 27." Churchill", Ashley Jackson, pub.by Quercus, NYC, London

2011, ISBN 978-1-62365-622-5 28." Churchill and Empire", by Lawrence James pub. by Pegasus Books. NYC, London 2004 29. "The Cinema of Central Europe", pub. Wallflower Press, London 2004, ISBN 1-904764-20-7 30. Sergei Eisenstein's," Ivan the Terrible" (1944-46) 31." Diary for My Children", Marza Meszaros-Hungarian Director 1982 32." The Good Soldier', 33. "Loves of a Blonde, "by Milos foreman, Director (1965) 34.'Closely Watched Trains",1967 Czech Film

PERSONAL STATEMENT

I worked in Studio City as an Executive Producer/Director for a Company, which I formed in 2003 called Odyessey IV Films Inc. It was on the impetus of my actors, at CSUN Northridge, who enjoyed a play which I wrote and produced on their stage. They told me to "just go for it" like the Nike ad. So I formed a sole proprietorship for five years which become a corporation in 2008.Our first action feature film," The Vanguard"2009 was distributed by Quantum Releasing in Burbank to seven European Nations including but not limited to; Germany, Italy, France and the Czech Republic. After a Director's Final cut edition was released later, it won a Special Director's Award at the "LA Movie Awards" International competition complete with a gold statuette.

We are currently working on two action features; one about Ireland, the other based on the novel, "The Sons of the South". They will be filmed in 2017-2018.

My educational background includes two Master's degrees, the first I attained at Dominican University, in Florence, Italy in 1980.It is out of the campus Rosary College, in Fiesole, Italy near the Villa Schifanoia. It is on the far side of the hill of the Villa I Tatti owned by the Berenson's, used by Harvard Graduates.

Later I attended California State University Northridge in Northridge, California for a second Master's in Mass Communication/Screenwriting which I completed in 2006.

We as a company immediately produced "The Vanguard."

My prior professions include running a fine art gallery, Odyessey II at Factory Place in Los Angeles.

Also, I worked as Director of Exhibitions for Orange County Center for Contemporary art in Santa Ana in 1980-1982.

Printed in the United States
By Bookmasters